From
Reading
to Math

From
Reading
<u>to</u>Math

HOW BEST PRACTICES IN LITERACY CAN
MAKE YOU A BETTER MATH TEACHER
GRADES K–5

MAGGIE SIENA

MATH SOLUTIONS • SAUSALITO, CALIFORNIA, USA

Math Solutions
150 Gate 5 Road
Sausalito, CA 94965
www.mathsolutions.com

Library of Congress Cataloging-in-Publication Data

CIP is on file with the Library of Congress.

ISBN 978-1-935099-04-8

EDITOR: *Jamie Cross*
PRODUCTION: *Melissa L. Inglis-Elliott*
COVER AND INTERIOR DESIGN: *Jenny Jensen Greenleaf*
COVER ILLUSTRATION: *Craig Shuttlewood/"Addition Demonstrated
        with Fruit"/Getty Images*
AUTHOR PHOTO: *Ken Schles*
COMPOSITION: *Macmillan Publishing Solutions*

Printed in the United States of America on acid-free paper
14 13 12 10 09   SB   1 2 3 4 5

A Message from Math Solutions

We at Math Solutions believe that teaching math well calls for increasing our understanding of the math we teach, seeking deeper insights into how children learn mathematics, and refining our lessons to best promote students' learning.

Math Solutions shares classroom-tested lessons and teaching expertise from our faculty of professional development instructors as well as from other respected math educators. Our publications are part of the nationwide effort we've made since 1984 that now includes

- more than five hundred face-to-face professional development programs each year for teachers and administrators in districts across the country;
- annually publishing professional development books, now totaling more than seventy titles and spanning the teaching of all math topics in kindergarten through grade 8;
- four series of videos for teachers, plus a video for parents, that show math lessons taught in actual classrooms;
- on-site visits to schools to help refine teaching strategies and assess student learning; and
- free online support, including grade-level lessons, book reviews, inservice information, and district feedback, all in our *Math Solutions Online Newsletter.*

For information about all of the products and services we have available, please visit our website at *www.mathsolutions.com.* You can also contact us to discuss math professional development needs by calling (800) 868-9092 or by sending an email to *info@mathsolutions.com.*

We're always eager for your feedback and interested in learning about your particular needs. We look forward to hearing from you.

mathsolutions.com

To all my teachers, past and present, with gratitude.

Brief Contents

Contents

Acknowledgments

I t takes a village to write a book. Through the long and fascinating process of writing this one, I have been fortunate to have the help of many wise, patient, and thoughtful people. I am indebted to Marilyn Burns, who has inspired me (and legions of teachers) to think deeply about teaching and mathematics. Toby Gordon's insight and seemingly endless patience helped me nurture an idea into a book. Maryann Wickett read each chapter with a warmly critical eye and offered faultless feedback. Jamie Cross edited the text masterfully and Melissa Inglis-Elliott guided the typed text into a bound book.

I am also indebted to the many brilliant teachers whose ideas I pass on here: my teachers from the Lucille M. Nixon Elementary School (circa 1970); Anna Switzer, Lucy West, and my many colleagues at PS 234; the staff members of PS 150, who remind me every day what dedication to children really looks like; Math Solutions's teaching consultants, so exceptionally knowledgeable about mathematics teaching and so incredibly funny to boot; the educational giants whose brilliant work provides guideposts for my teaching, among them Richard Allington, Cathy Fosnot, Stephanie Harvey, Ellin Keene, Jon Saphier, Frank Smith, and Diane Snowball.

Finally, I am grateful to my husband, Ken. He has been patient, too, plus a good cook and confidant. What can top that?

Introduction

I f you have been successful in teaching children to read and write, you have the skills, tools, and strategies you need to succeed in teaching children math. If you are a great language teacher, you can be a great math teacher, too. Though they may seem to come from Venus and Mars, mathematics and literacy are as alike as they are different. We read, write, and think mathematically to make sense of the world we live in, and to see, express, and celebrate its beauty. They are languages we speak, and while they may both be inscribed on paper, they both unfold in the thinker's mind.

This book explores how effective teaching of math looks a lot like effective teaching of literacy. It is also about what math teachers can learn from literacy teaching. First, look at how the fundamental bits and pieces of mathematics and literacy, numerals and letters, are alike. In both cases, these marks on paper carry specific meanings to be decoded. Because the languages of mathematics and literacy both have written codes to be read, we can use what we know about decoding words, such as drawing on context, to help our young mathematicians make sense of numbers. Vocabulary and fluency, key to success in literacy, also play significant parts as young learners break the written mathematics code.

What you know about reading comprehension is especially useful in teaching and learning mathematics. While literacy and mathematics both depend on the learner's ability to decode symbols, why bother unless the results are meaningful? Contrary to the classic saying *Yours is not to question why; just invert and multiply,* it is not enough to invert and multiply—we need to reason why. Recent work in reading comprehension by scores of literacy educators provides math teachers with valuable strategies for digging deeply into mathematics meaning. By explicitly teaching students to use such powerful cognitive tools as predicting, questioning, inferring, and synthesizing to comprehend the mathematics they are learning, we help them deepen their mathematical understanding.

The pedagogical approaches you use to teach literacy can also maximize mathematics learning. First, the ways effective literacy teachers organize their classrooms for successful reading and writing instruction offer powerful strategies to math teachers. Print-rich environments, daily practice in reading and writing, and integration of literacy activities into the life of the classroom are all practices that math teachers can borrow. In addition, the workshop model, an effective structure for teaching and learning reading and writing, has much to share with the math class. The thinking literacy teachers have done about direct instruction, small-group work, guided reading, and independent practice in reading and writing can help math teachers structure powerful lessons that are relevant, challenging, and engaging to students.

Literacy teachers have also developed practical and effective strategies for assessment that math teachers can learn from. Look at two significant contributions especially useful for math teachers: running records (which give us a glimpse into what a reader is doing as she reads) and conferring (which helps us see what readers and writers are thinking about). After all, though we do care what a child's answer to a math problem is, what we really need to know is how he arrived at it and how he was thinking about the question. We benefit from sitting by students and recording what they are doing in mathematics and by talking with them about how they decide to do it.

Finally, reading teachers have a lot to teach math teachers about helping struggling learners. At the top of the list is a commitment to helping all children succeed. When we are teaching mathematics, we need to be sure we have that same commitment and are not secretly subscribing to a belief in the missing math gene.

Of course, in most elementary classrooms these literacy and math teachers are one and the same person. This is me, the literacy teacher, and now here I am, the math teacher. Yet sometimes it does feel like we are taking off the literacy hat to put on the math cap when we shift from one subject to another. This book suggests that this shift is not as dramatic as it sometimes seems, and that we can bring much of what makes us great at teaching reading and writing to our teaching of math.

Over all, this book is about teaching. But it is also about thinking. It is concerned with the kinds of thinking learners do when they engage in reading, writing, and mathematics as well as the kinds of thinking teachers do to understand our subjects, our students, and our craft.

This book is ultimately about learning. It looks at how students learn, and how we, as teachers, can nurture their potential. It is also about our learning, which means questioning what we think about literacy, teaching, and mathematics, looking at how the teaching and learning of these topics overlap, and learning how we can bring our strengths as reading and writing teachers into the math class.

The Role of the Teacher

Imagine you are conferring one-on-one with a student during reading workshop. You are working on a strategy with her and she's really getting it. You glance up and see that the rest of the students, either in pairs or individually, are engaged in their reading. There's a positive energy in the room, and you smile at this triumph. But do you stop to think about why everything is going so smoothly? What is the root of this success?

If you are reading this book, you are most likely a teacher. And if you are a teacher, you are well aware of the dizzying list of skills requiring your proficiency. Part of what makes teaching so interesting and rewarding is that it is a multidimensional task. It requires the skills of a sheepdog and an air traffic controller, a professional organizer and a child psychologist, a parent and a motivational speaker. You need to know both your content area (or areas, which for elementary educators may easily number six) and pedagogical strategies, both of which are constantly growing bodies of knowledge. And you must never lose sight of the real lives and needs of the young students in your care. No wonder teachers have the summers off!

The good news is that we teach best when we see ourselves as learners. After all, everything we know is subject to change, and we are certainly learning more about, well, everything as time goes on. This is true for both the field of education and general knowledge. For example, when I was in school, dinosaurs were leathery-looking animals that were just plain extinct. Now scientists have uncovered evidence that at least some of these creatures had feathers and evolved over time into birds. This means today's birds are descended from dinosaurs! Our learning never stops.

Moreover, we inspire and teach our students when we embrace ourselves as learners, too. Effective teachers convey knowledge, embody values, excite curiosity, and never lose sight of the fact that they are not teaching reading or math—they are teaching humans. Teachers are, without a doubt, the single most important factor in successful learning. It follows that you, the teacher, will play the most important role in your students' success in math. As important as curriculum, assessment tools, and a well-supplied and well-supported classroom may be, without an effective teacher at the helm to make sense of all the variables in the classroom, these components amount to very little. Teachers know this. It is why we choose this path.

The question is: How can we make the path we've chosen as smooth as possible? How can we continue to support and enrich our learning while simultaneously ensuring that the learning of our students is maximized? In my quest to do everything, I've returned to the saving grace: I'm a learner, too. And what I've learned is that we can become more effective teachers of mathematics by drawing from our successful experiences with teaching literacy. It's the art of lighting two candles with one flame.

In this first chapter, let's consider four qualities of literacy teaching that we can transfer to our role as math teachers: love of reading, active learning, a positive and passionate attitude, and differentiated instruction. We'll first look at each of these in the context of literacy teaching, then link them to math.

Love of Reading

First and foremost, let us pay homage to the read-aloud. Surely it is one of the most joyful times of the school day: reading wonderful books aloud to our young students gathered around us, their hungry minds devouring every word. We know that reading aloud is a highly successful instructional method, but that does not explain why it is so pleasurable or why students and teachers alike are often so eager for more (I can hear the daily groans when I put the bookmark in, indicating a closure to the day's read-aloud). The reason is simply that *we love reading.* When teachers read aloud, we are teaching our students to love reading, too. This is critical! Becoming a reader is hard work: As young children, we must overcome the challenges of decoding, and as we grow, we must learn ever more sophisticated strategies for understanding ever more complex texts. This work asks for effort, and we are far more likely to exert effort when we love what we are doing. We succeed in teaching readers when we invite them to share our love of reading.

Active Learning

Successful literacy teachers are active readers and writers. We study our own reading and writing, and we share our challenges and successes with our students. This may mean delving into genres we have previously avoided (nonfiction for the fiction fan or poetry for the prose lover) or consciously experimenting with comprehension strategies. We also study the reading and writing habits of our students, asking such questions as What does she like to read? Why is spelling so hard for him? What strengths do my students bring to the table?

A Positive and Passionate Attitude

We succeed in bringing our students into the world of literacy when we embrace curiosity, tolerance, open-mindedness, and critical thinking. We do this by inviting learners to observe our own thinking processes and by sharing our thoughts about their learning. We also do this by setting high expectations for literacy learning and respecting children's learning processes. When the state of New York adopted a performance standard requiring all fourth graders to read at least twenty-five books, Francesca struggled to meet this goal. She was a reader whose capacity to comprehend far outstripped her ability to decode; she often opted to read books that were just right in content but difficult to decode, and it took time to get through them. She worried that she would not meet the twenty-five-book standard. I wanted to support Francesca's goal of reading twenty-five challenging texts, and I respected her determination and perseverance. Working together, we identified a number of shorter texts that stimulated her thinking, including a couple of collections of poetry, and found some great books that were at her decoding level.

Differentiated Instruction

By understanding our own strengths, weaknesses, and interests, and studying those of our students, we develop an appreciation of the complex nature of literacy learning and know that each learner has a unique learning profile. Effective teachers use this knowledge to plan the best instruction for each student: appropriate grouping or partnerships, texts that delight a student or push him further, specific strategy instruction, and more. In a nutshell, effective teachers know their students. It is also important for teachers to really know themselves. My insights into myself as a learner (I prefer fiction, hate drafting, need to think about spelling patterns, like a little noise when I'm writing, and tend to overcomplicate sentences) allow me to develop insights into others as well as keep in mind that there is a vast array of conditions that work best for other writers.

Effective teachers bring these same qualities to math teaching. We strive to convey the beauty and pleasure of mathematics, learn alongside our students, model positive values, reflect, and help our students excel at and enjoy mathematics.

But here is the catch: For many of us, math does *not* hold the same pleasure that reading does. A lot of teachers simply don't like math, and some even fear it. Some teachers were not particularly successful as math students and stopped taking it as soon as they could. Teaching math is a solemn duty, approached with respect and some trepidation. Those of us who have not had the best experiences in mathematics still understand how important it is to our students, and we strive to teach it well. But when we teach it without enthusiasm or curiosity, we should not be surprised to find that our students feel the same way.

The first lesson we should take from literacy teaching is to *fall in love with math*—at least at little bit—so we can honestly teach out of curiosity and enthusiasm. Though this may seem a bit touchy-feely, if you swap out *math* for *reading,* it sounds perfectly natural. After all, while it is oddly commonplace for people to claim they hate math, it is nearly unthinkable for an adult to say the same about reading.

If the idea of falling in love with math sounds impossible to you, my guess is that you are affected by a math education that failed you.

You may have found fractions confusing and struggled to learn how to add, subtract, multiply, or divide them. Long division was baffling and algebra, nearly impossible. You felt like an outsider in math class and envied those children who seemed to get it so easily (they must have had the mythical math gene). Because traditional procedures reliably produced correct answers, and were likely the focus of the curriculum, you worked hard to master them. You probably did this mostly through rote practice and got more pleasure out of succeeding on tests than playing with numbers.

If this is you, you need to rediscover math. And lucky you—you have a golden opportunity to do so. Remember, the most effective teachers are lead learners. So learn with your students. You already know the math they are studying better than they do, so you are one crucial step ahead. You can afford to let down your guard and investigate with your students. The mathematics games and investigations written for children are often very engaging for adults as well, and teachers who have been alienated from math are often delighted to discover how—dare I say it?—*fun* math can be. And here's the secret: If you are honest with yourself, you will never stop learning with your students. The mathematics underpinning even the most elementary concepts are so rich—the possibilities for learning so abundant—that you are bound to encounter students who will push your thinking.

I offer the following advice for teachers everywhere, no matter how you feel about math:

My Advice to Math Teachers

Examine how you feel about math.

Try out new strategies.

Make mistakes—publicly.

Really try to understand your students, and don't be surprised when you can't.

Find colleagues or mentors to learn with.

Above all, remember you are human in a human endeavor.

Examine how you feel about math.

Examine your own beliefs about math, and think about changing them. If you really believe that mathematics can be learned only by those blessed with the math gene, think again. Yes, numeracy may come more easily to some, but since mathematics understanding can enter through many avenues (spatial, linguistic, and numeric), there is an in for every learner. Find out how *you* learn best: Alone, with a partner, or in a group? Playing with manipulatives or scribbling thoughts down on paper? Working through reliable procedures or performing trial and error? For every preference you have, there is a learner with an opposite preference. Look for preferences in your students. Next, consider your teaching preferences, keeping in mind the fact that no one practice or approach will succeed with all learners (this is probably one of the few absolutes in education). Any piece of rigid thinking is dangerous and should be examined. We have all been the victims of dogma in education and should strive to avoid being dogmatic. Read current research and continue to do your own fieldwork: study your students, and study yourself.

Try out new strategies.

No matter how comfortable you are with math, there is always something new for you to try; the wider your mathematics repertoire, the better you will understand your students and the math they are learning. While studying mathematics teaching with mathematics educator Cathy Fosnot, I learned a novel approach to multiplication, based on the fact that if you halve one factor and double the other, the product remains the same. That is, 8×6 yields the same answer as 4×12 and as 2×24. As cool as I thought this was, I fancied myself as pretty good at multiplication and saw little need to adopt a new strategy. However, upon reflection I recognized that this attitude was limiting at best and anti-learning at worst. I began to consciously apply the halving and doubling strategy to multiplication problems. I quickly learned this strategy was not much use with problems like 39×11, but it sure made 12×75 a snap! With just a couple of mental steps, I easily solved that problem in my head: 6×150 is doable, and 3×300 is a piece of cake. Not only was this getting fun, but I was seeing the benefit of being more open-minded. Next stop: subtraction.

Make mistakes—publicly.

Where math is concerned, teachers tend to be focused on right answers. That is not a bad thing: after all, mathematics is beautiful in its precision, and it is important that our students know how to get correct answers quickly and efficiently. But, as I have already said, right answers are not the be-all and the end-all. It is the thinking behind answers, right and wrong, that is most important, and it is often said that there is more to be learned from wrong answers than from right ones. Our role as teachers is to dedicate the classroom to *thinking* rather than to answers. Learning to think requires a lot of mistake making. Show your students that mistakes are valuable sources of learning by being public about yours. I am not suggesting you make fake mistakes. Children are very perceptive and hate when we are condescending. If you are like me, you will have ample opportunities to show off your real errors. When you make mistakes, model the type of respectful behavior that you expect students to have. Don't make embarrassed exclamations ("That was stupid of me!") or denigrate your own potential ("I'm not very good at math."); you are modeling how you want your students to treat themselves and others when they make an error. "Isn't that interesting," you might appropriately say. "At first I thought this, but I realized I made a mistake."

Really try to understand your students, and don't be surprised when you can't.

Frankly, it can be positively bedeviling to make sense of others' reasoning, and when the others in question are a few decades younger than you—and less experienced in communicating their mental processes—it can be nearly impossible. Don't give up! When you say, "I'm curious about how you got that answer," make sure your students know you mean it. Don't understand their first explanation? Ask again. Still don't understand? Ask if another student can explain. Offer your students tools (manipulatives, the chalkboard) to represent the answer visually. Still getting nowhere, and losing your audience? Make a date to talk about it later—and keep it. Children are always trying to make sense of things, and it is our obligation and privilege to help them. We benefit, too. Not only do we find out more about how children think, but we may learn an approach or an idea that we have never seen before.

Find colleagues or mentors to learn with.

Find a teacher next door, a math coach, or a professional book on the topic of mathematics teaching. When teachers of literacy are enthusiastic about their work, they seek outside stimulation to feed their thinking and their practice. Give yourself the same gift in the field of mathematics. Play a math game with a spouse, look over student work with a fellow teacher, share your confusion with a staff developer or coach, attend a mathematics education workshop or conference, and turn to a trusted professional book. Taking these actions can serve to feed your learning quest, stimulate your interest in math, and keep you up-to-date in the field.

Above all, remember you are human in a human endeavor.

H. L. Mencken wrote, "There is always an easy solution to every human problem—neat, plausible, and wrong" (1949). Mathematics teaching has its share of problems. A short, simple solution is bound to be wrong. Any possible solutions (definitely long and complex) lie within us. Teachers, each in their own classrooms with their own communities of learners, utilize all the understanding, skill, and attitude they can to improve education. To undertake this challenge, we must be accepting of failure (after all, Sigmund Freud named teaching as one of two impossible professions). We must keep in mind that we are likely to make mistakes and remain committed to learning from them. Like any journey, it is not the destination but the learning along the way that counts.

FROM READING TO MATH TO YOUR CLASSROOM

1. *What are strategies for teaching reading that you feel particularly confident with that you can adapt for teaching math?*

2. *What are aspects of math learning or teaching that you already enjoy? If you feel there are no enjoyable aspects, how might you find a way to fall in love with math?*

3. *Can you think of any lessons your students have taught you about math? Have you been open to letting them teach you?*

Decoding, Fluency, and Vocabulary

Have you ever had a student who just knew the answer to a math problem but couldn't explain why it was correct? Have you ever had a student arrive at a completely ridiculous answer to a math problem without realizing that it made no sense at all? It's likely that these students struggled with decoding math, computing fluently, or understanding math language.

When my daughter Julia entered kindergarten, she was poised to become a reader. She had fallen in love with books long before age five. Even as an active four-month-old whose legs just never stopped moving, she would gaze with rapt fascination at the board books we held before her. By five she had become extremely knowledgeable about books and their contents: information, stories, poems, and jokes. She knew how books were laid out, that they had authors and (often) illustrators. She knew that the text ran from left to right and how to turn the pages. She was a skilled predictor: she used her knowledge of the world and her growing understanding of how stories usually go to guess what words we would encounter and what would probably happen next. She could even identify a few words—important ones, like her name, *cat*, and *birthday*. Still, the code remained unbroken. She was not a reader—yet. She still needed to learn how to decode.

There is magic in reading. What else do you call the transformation of black squiggles into whole worlds, real and imagined? Marks on a page—mere marks—tell stories, express feelings, reveal secrets, and pass on our knowledge of the universe. Though an author casts a spell of one kind, the reader also makes magic. Where else do those marks become meaning but in the reader's mind? The reader-magician decodes, turning marks into words, then building those words into facts, ideas, feelings, and more.

Likewise, my daughter Julia entered kindergarten as a budding mathematician. She could describe the world in mathematical ways; her brother had more gummy bears, our orange cat was littler than the black one, her cracker was a square (then nibbled and—surprise!—a circle). Julia speculated about how many birthday presents she expected to receive (always lots, sometimes ten, and other times "forty-one a hundred and a thousand") and took care to carefully count out the six chocolate chips that she got each time we made cookies (her age plus one more). But she could not yet make true sense of the numbers she saw in print all around her—on the calendar, in our cookbooks, or painted on our front door. She had not broken that code, either.

Numerals and Letters: A Comparison

Both literacy and mathematics use written symbols to communicate meaning. If students cannot decode those symbols—that is, bring meaning to them—they will be unable to enter those very rich worlds of thinking. Numerals are similar to letters in many ways:

Numerals and Letters: The Similarities

SYMBOLS
Style and font aside, letters and numerals are written much the same way each time, though there is no connection between the way the symbols are shaped and their meanings. There is no *puh* in the shape of the letter P and there is nothing about the quantity five in the numeral 5. Any meaning that a child gives to symbols exists completely in the child's mind, not in the symbol itself.

(*continued*)

Numerals and Letters: The Similarities   (*continued*)

NAMES
Each letter and numeral has a name. Again, this name has nothing to do with the symbol's meaning or value. Knowing the letter name pronounced *why* doesn't help you read or write the letter Y, and the numeral name *three* is no help in discerning the meaning of the symbol 3.

LIMITED SETS
There is a limited set of both letters and numerals. English speakers use fifty-two letters (including upper-case and lowercase symbols) to write all words. We construct all numbers with the same ten digits (0, 1, 2, 3, 4, 5, 6, 7, 8, 9).

OTHER SYMBOLS
Both literacy and mathematics involve a number of other symbols. Reading and writing rely on punctuation and strategic use of capitalization. In mathematics we employ operation symbols ($+$, $-$, $\times$, $\div$) and relation symbols ($=$, $>$, $<$, and so on), use parentheses for punctuation, write numbers as superscripts for exponents, and, at times, even use letters.

REPRESENTATIONS
Each symbol can contribute to representing something beyond its shape or name. We combine letters to build words; we combine numerals to communicate quantities.

CONTEXT
Context counts: We can't be sure of the pronunciation of *read* until we see it in a sentence ("Are you going to read that book I read yesterday?") or the meaning of the word *fluke* unless we see it in context. When we see 5 on its own, we visualize one quantity. When it joins two zeros in 500, we imagine quite another.

Decoding: From Reading to Math

There are also significant differences in the decoding involved in literacy and mathematics. Decoding in reading is mastered once; learning to decode in mathematics continues throughout formal schooling (and maybe beyond!). Both reading and doing mathematics (arithmetic, in particular) require us to take note of symbols and quickly—virtually instantly—assign those symbols with meaning. This process starts slowly and, with practice over time, speeds up.

In reading, decoding is, paradoxically, both complex and straightforward. Decoding is a gatekeeper skill, and once mastered, it serves readers their whole lives. No matter how challenging, in literacy, learning to decode is a finite task. Though letters function in a few different ways—for example, as handy labels *Group A* or *Brand X*—in the world of literacy, for the most part letters represent sounds and are used to form the unique arrangements we call words. However, the decoding that is involved in reading is not by any means obvious. Letters may represent a number of different sounds, depending on the words in which they appear. P *puhs* when it is part of *potato*, and it *ffs* when it joins with H to start *phone*. Decoding words proves challenging, even daunting, to some students (there are at least eight ways to spell the long E sound, for example). It certainly takes skill to teach it well. However, because effective readers do not tend to rely on sounding out as a decoding strategy, it is not necessary to learn all eight spelling patterns for the long E sound to decode the words that include them.

Unless they face a serious learning challenge, most children develop the ability to decode text in the first few years of formal schooling. Accomplished readers cease sounding out words and may not even "hear" words when they are reading silently in their heads. In fact, once the code it broken, readers may pay very little attention to the sound of letters at all. It seems that just having the first and last letter in place is enough for most readers to swiftly decode. Try reading the following sentence:

> *Its anizamg how erftofellssy plopee can eevn raed wdors taht are tihs srcbalmed!*

Fluent readers still have a lot to learn about reading—that is, bringing meaning to the printed page—but once they can decode, they can concentrate on comprehending, comparing, interpreting, and criticizing.

The scope of decoding in mathematics is quite another matter. The mathematics learner faces one decoding challenge after another: new symbols are introduced (variables, the different symbols that mean *divide*), old ones are used in new ways (numbers used in fractions and exponents), and positions take on new meanings ($2x$ means 2 times x). To keep up in mathematics, the learner must constantly expand and revise his decoding skills. There is no one gatekeeper skill that gives the learner access to mathematics the way decoding does in literacy. Consider the comparison:

What We Decode in Reading	What We Decode in Doing Math (an incomplete list!)
words	whole numbers (quantity associated with numerals and place value)
letters used as labels	
punctuation	integers (including negative numbers)
	operation signs
	equivalence signs
	rational and irrational numbers (fractions and decimals)
	percents
	exponents
	variables
	graphs
	notation used in measurement (350°, 6'5")
	notation used in geometry (e.g., symbol indicating right angle)
	notation used in trigonometry and calculus

In addition to the scope of decoding, symbols in mathematics are more complex. Even the very first mathematics symbols a young learner decodes are more complex than the letters that make up written language. A number, on its own, stands for much more than any single letter does, and it may convey many complex meanings. Take 5 for example. It can represent *quantity*: five pennies, five beluga whales, or five marshmallows. It can represent *position*: the fifth customer on line or the fifth seat in a row. It can represent a *measurement*: 5 minutes, 5 feet of ribbon, or 5 pounds of cheese. And, of course, it can be a *label*: group number 5, or the 5 in a PIN.

In elementary school mathematics, the emphasis is on thinking about numbers as representing quantities, often in the context of arithmetic. Numerals take on whole new meanings when positioned with other numerals. Again, let's look at 5. While it can represent five pennies or whales, it may actually mean fifty, or five hundred, or five million, depending on its position in a string of numerals—50, or 500, or 5,000,000. Or it can be part of a fraction or a decimal and refer to fifths or tenths—$\frac{1}{5}$ or 0.5. It can be used as a factor to mean groups of some quantity: for example, 5×4 means five groups of four. Or it can be used as an exponent and tell how many times to multiply a number by itself—2^5 is two to the fifth power. Think about what a young person needs to do to break this code: she needs to relate a mark to a name *and* know something about its many possible meanings. That's a lot!

The numeral 24 gives us other ideas to talk about. We can talk about the evenness of twenty-four, its factors, its location on the number line and 1–100 chart, and its use in measurement. We can talk about having 24 cents (not so much) or twenty-four mosquito bites (too many by far). Twenty-four is a complex idea, and both school and life experiences have helped us learn to decode it in many ways, depending on its context.

Decoding Reading

Meaning

In reading, learning to decode begins and ends with meaning. That is, making meaning is always our goal and often our most effective strategy. Next, syntax and phonics support decoding. Effective readers attend to all three, and when they read, consciously or unconsciously they are poised with the questions Does that make sense? Does that sound right? Does that look right?

First, meaning (conveyed through context and pictures) provides powerful motivation for decoding. Readers don't just want to get good at reading; they want to find out what happened to Harry Potter! Meaning helps us anticipate vocabulary (we know what words to expect in a pirate story) and suggests what will come next. Beginning texts also provide picture cues, helping students focus on what the book is about. A young reader gets support for reading

"I put on my hat" when there is an accompanying photograph. Even a very early reader may be able to read the big word *elephant* when there is picture support or if the book is about African mammals. Children who know a lot about the world—who have visited zoos, museums, stores, parks; seen great movies or TV; and been read to from a huge range of books—are well prepared to use meaning as a decoding skill.

Syntax

Syntax, the grammar of English, supports young readers as well. Because language flows in a way that is generally predictable, and context limits what words we might expect to see in any given text, even beginning readers can predict what words might come next in a simple, unfamiliar text. Notice how often you are ready with the next word of a sentence you are reading even before you have turned a page—and how infrequently you are wrong. Children who are often read to can read for themselves the three words that follow "Once . . ." When children have been immersed in language—listening to and speaking with adults, hearing stories read and reread aloud—they are prepared to use this decoding strategy.

Phonics

Phonic cues also play an important role in decoding text. When meaning and syntax narrow down what an unfamiliar word might be, letter cues help readers decide the matter. Young learners reading Karen Pandell's book *I Love You, Sun, I Love You, Moon* (2003), are supported by the repeating text, "I love you, _____" and helpful picture cues. However, in order to decode "I love you, rabbit," beginning readers will need letter cues to decide if the right word is *bunny* or *rabbit*.

Young readers can also make excellent use of letter sounds, especially initial sounds, or *onsets*, and familiar spelling patterns, or *rimes*, such as *-ake* or *-all*. Children who know letter names and the sounds they commonly make and have played with rhyming are well equipped to use phonic cues to decode. The ability to rhyme is not only fun, but it is a powerful reading skill. In fact, familiarity with nursery rhymes is a reliable predictor of initial success in reading. When children learn the onset-rime decoding strategy, they can use their knowledge of the word *cat* to also read the words *hat, sat, rat,* and *mat*.

Meaning, Syntax, and Phonics

These three components of decoding—meaning, syntax, and phonics—work together beautifully. When teachers provide explicit instruction about how to use meaning, syntax, and phonics cues to decode, the stage is set for decoding with comprehension. Yet even before this can be done, children must

◆ learn the letters of the alphabet and the sounds they most commonly represent;

◆ be able to recognize and create rhymes;

◆ have some fund of general knowledge (reading is made much, much harder when readers have no prior knowledge of a topic);

◆ build rich vocabularies (narrowing the truly unknown words they will encounter);

◆ know something about stories and story language; and

◆ expect the things they read to mean something *and* expect to be satisfied by that meaning.

Though for many fortunate children the way is paved at home, sometimes teachers need to lay this important groundwork.

Decoding Mathematics

As in literacy, meaning plays a critical role in decoding mathematics. Since making meaning is important both as a strategy and as the ultimate goal of doing mathematics, learning is supported when symbols are presented in a context. I can help my young students understand what 5 means by giving them opportunities to count five objects (over and over again). But at some point I will need to tell them, "This is how we write five." Similarly, my older students started making sense of fractions by dividing "brownies" into equal shares and making and labeling paper-strip fraction kits. However, I could not expect them to construct—on their own—the way fractions are written.

Different kinds of knowledge make up mathematical understanding. In *About Teaching Mathematics,* Marilyn Burns writes, "Children need to learn mathematical concepts and see relationships between these concepts. Because mathematical concepts and relations are constructed by people and exist only in their minds, children must construct these concepts and relationships in their own minds" (2007, 24). She goes on to say that some of what children need to learn they cannot construct for themselves. The symbolism we use to represent mathematical ideas—numbers, operations and relations signs, for example—is a social convention. Social knowledge comes from outside the learner. Though children will need many concrete experiences to learn what five means, someone will need to tell them how to represent it symbolically.

Children often enter kindergarten being able to "count" the numbers one to ten, sometimes higher, generally tripping up in those challenging teens. Their counting resembles the singsong way they often chant the alphabet, with the famous letter *elemenuhpee*. While they are demonstrating some important knowledge, it is not yet fully understood. At this point, they often still know little about the numbers they are saying. As teachers, we help students develop the conceptual understanding underlying the symbolic representations they have memorized. One way we do this is by giving students opportunities to explore the concepts and quantities the symbols represent in context.

In literacy, contexts for this work include lists of rhyming words; books, stories, and poems; and labeled pictures. In mathematics, contexts include number lines and charts; games of all kinds (including math games, board games, and Yahtzee); number stories; and labeled pictures. We learn to decode numbers in the daily context of our classrooms.

Sample Contexts: Reading	Sample Contexts: Math
lists of rhyming words	number lines
books	charts
stories	games
poems	number stories
labeled pictures	labeled pictures

One group of first graders I taught demonstrated the usefulness of number contexts to support their budding number sense. It was the afternoon of the first day of school for my combined kindergarten and first-grade class. The kindergartners went home early (exhausted) and I found myself alone with my group of "big kids." We gathered in the meeting area, and I asked who would like to count how many kids were left. Everyone was eager to accept my invitation, and out of the dozen hands waving before me I chose Teddy's. Standing up, Teddy marched confidently but randomly around the rug, tapping his classmates on the head (not so lightly in Kate's opinion). "One, two, three, four, five, six, seven, eight, nine, ten, eleven, twelve, thirteen," Teddy counted, matching words for taps, ending with a decisive tap on his own head.

"You missed me!" Neal said.

"And you got me two times," added Miranda.

"Me, too," Meshawn said.

"Would you like to try again?" I asked Teddy.

Undeterred, Teddy began to start over, then stopped. "Wait a minute," he said. "You sit here," he told Neal, "and you sit here," he told Askia, pointing next to Neal. Teddy took his time, clearly enjoying this chance to tell his classmates what to do. His classmates gamely complied as he arranged them in a rough circle. He returned to Neal and began tapping and counting again, this time with increased seriousness and decreased speed: "One. Two. Three. Four. Five. Six. Seven. Eight. Nine. Ten. Eleven. Plus me—that makes twelve!" He ended again with a tap on his own head. Enthusiastic applause; his classmates approved of both his strategy and his result.

"What happened?" I asked. "Teddy got thirteen the first time he counted and twelve the second time."

"It's twelve," said Askia, "because Teddy counted us wrong the first time and the second time he counted real carefully—one, two, three, four, five, six, seven, eight, nine, ten, eleven, twelve." Askia pointed to the kids in the circle as she counted. Teddy and Askia had both demonstrated sound number sense!

"Would you like to write twelve?" I asked Askia. She took the chalk and hesitantly stood before the board. We all waited patiently. Though it was the first day of school, the kids had spent kindergarten with me, and they knew Askia sometimes needed time to think. Askia wrote *21* on the board then turned to her classmates, a quizzical look on her face. Some kids shook their heads "no"; others stared blankly. Askia turned back and wrote *12* next to the 21. "I'm not sure which way it goes," she said with a shrug.

"It's that one," Pat called out, pointing to 12. Pat was very bright, if a bit impatient; there was an undertone of *Duh!* to his answer. Though there were uncertain faces among his classmates, there was no dissent. Pat had a reputation in the class: he was good at math. Still, just because his answer carried authority with his classmates, it didn't mean they understood why his was the right choice.

"How can we be sure?" I asked.

"It just is," said Pat. "Twelve goes one and then a two." Pat spoke with confidence. He was sure what the number twelve looked like, but had no mathematical reason why it was right. Because he was still constructing an understanding of place value, he was relying on the social knowledge he had acquired.

"Is there something in our classroom we can look at to help us decide if Pat's answer makes sense?" I asked. I waited as the kids looked around, some purposefully, others with growing restlessness. I wasn't going to have their attention for much longer.

Donata timidly raised her hand. "The number line?" she offered. At my invitation, Donata stood to show how the number line might help the class nail down the identity of the illusive number 12. "See," she said, pointing with the ruler, "it counts up one, two, three, four, five, six, seven, eight, nine, ten, eleven, then there's twelve. So that's twelve."

There were nods and expressions of satisfaction on most of the young faces looking up at me. Michelle and Marco looked a bit lost. I made a mental note to check in with them later. Satisfied with our impromptu investigation, I turned the class's attention to the illustrated list of math activities from which they would choose. All the children needed to do independent exploration to develop and extend their understanding of these fascinating numbers in the teens.

This context asked a lot of these young mathematicians. So much is embedded in the familiar counting sequence; it is easy for adults—accomplished counters with decades of counting experience—to forget all the skills and complex conceptual ideas involved.

In this instance, Teddy showed he had these concepts under his belt:

- he could count easily to twelve (the rote counting sequence);

- he knew that the last number he said represented the total counted (cardinality);

- he knew that to get an accurate count he needed to count each person once and only once (one-to-one correspondence);

- he knew that his tagging and word saying should happen at the same time (synchrony); and

- he knew that eleven plus one more—himself—made a total of twelve (hierarchical inclusion).

He still had skills to develop, but he showed he was on his way in his reliable strategy to ensure he counted everyone in the class. What he and his classmates still needed to work on was the integration of the quantity twelve and the word *twelve* with the written number 12.

The symbolic formation of the number twelve is something Teddy and his classmates could not construct, the way they would have to construct the association between the word or symbol and the quantity. After all, there are many ways in which human beings have represented that quantity orally and in writing. Teddy and his classmates needed to be told what twelve looked like when written as a number. The kids had likely seen a 12 in some context before starting kindergarten, but most were still unable to reliably connect that symbol with the name and quantity.

All through their mathematics education, students continue learning how to decode mathematical symbols. By looking at what these symbols represent in a number of contexts, children can build a robust understanding of their rich meanings.

Fluency: From Reading to Math

While fluency is a goal in many curriculum areas, including writing, reading, foreign languages, and mathematical computation, it seems to have a different meaning for each. Fluent spellers write words rapidly and accurately; fluent readers read words smoothly and with natural inflection; fluent language speakers can converse easily using a range of vocabulary approximating a native speaker's; and students are called computationally fluent when they can arrive at accurate solutions for arithmetic problems with ease (though it does not necessarily mean that they are good at executing the traditional algorithms—these are just a few of many efficient strategies).

What is common is the sense that the nuts and bolts of a particular subject have been mastered. When students are fluent in the key skills relevant to decoding in reading, writing, and mathematics, they can focus on the big picture: What is this book really about? What do I want to say in this poem? What am I finding out about perimeter (or probability or measurement)?

Fluency and Reading

Fluent readers demonstrate that they can recognize and read the words in a text and that they have a sense of story language. Fluent readers also tend to have a higher reading rate, which means they can read faster than nonfluent readers. It is well documented that the volume of reading one does is the number one factor in good reading progress. Fluency does not in itself create meaning, nor does it guarantee that readers are comprehending well. However, because fluency is so highly correlated with comprehension in reading, teachers have made it a goal to help all students read smoothly, flowingly, and with good intonation. We help students develop fluency by having them read appropriately challenging books that are interesting, having them read silently (and without interruption), and giving them opportunities to frequently reread favorite texts (Allington 2006).

Students who do not read fluently tend to be struggling readers. They may have poor or limited decoding skills (including overemphasis on word-by-word phonic strategies), little sense of how story language usually goes, and inadequate understanding that what they are reading should mean something.

A struggling fourth-grade reader perfectly illustrated what happens when students don't expect reading to be meaningful. Though Lamar was an articulate and confident speaker as well as a competent decoder, his reading was choppy and mechanical. He also disdained reading; he would rather do almost anything else. His big break-through came when he was finally matched to the right book, in terms of both interest and reading level. "Hey," he said one day, "this book is great. It's like watching TV!" It was clear that he had not yet realized that reading could be that engaging and that effortless. When you are really reading (and not just decoding), the story unfolds around you, and you are free to do the same kind of thinking you would do when watching a mystery show or a nature program. As you read, thoughts like "I think the thief was the big brother—definitely the big brother," and "Run, baby wildebeest, run! Get away from those lions!" stream through your mind. Just imagine what reading was like before Lamar got it. Reading without understanding—and engagement—is boring and frustrating. When Lamar began to expect stories to make sense, his oral reading also began to make sense.

Fluency and Mathematics

Fluency plays an important role in mathematics as well. Though it is not sufficient to be able to compute quickly or rapidly recall facts, it is hard to get down to the business of thinking mathematically when you are struggling with computation and facts. Conversely, a student cannot be called truly fluent when there is no other recourse to deciding if an answer is accurate than reliance on a well-practiced procedure. When students are really computationally fluent, they can quickly arrive at a solution and decide on their own if it is reasonable. As with Lamar, to become truly fluent, students need to have an expectation that the math they are doing rapidly will make sense to them.

Lack of fluency, then, is the bad marriage of weak basic skills and poor attention to meaning. You can address problems in fluency by doing the following:

Addressing Fluency Problems in Math

Help students to know what good understanding means. Just as Lamar needed to know that reading should be at least as rewarding an experience as watching TV, he needs to know that the math he is doing should make sense, and that he should get that satisfying payoff of doing math with understanding.

(*continued*)

Addressing Fluency Problems in Math   (*continued*)

Make sure students have the opportunity to do work that is challenging, but not too hard. Students build fluency (and the corresponding confidence) when they meet challenges successfully, again and again.

Address serious problems in basic understandings. In literacy, students need strong working knowledge of sound-symbol correspondence and good sight vocabulary. In math, students need good sense of number and quick recall of basic facts.

Fluency is a strong indicator of confidence as well. When Tasha was in third grade, she struggled in math. Because she was such a keen and analytic thinker, it made no sense to me that she was struggling. However, it made perfect sense to her. "I'm not good in math," she said. "I just can't do it."

"Yes, you can," I'd think. "I know you can. You just lack the confidence to discover that."

Tasha's breakthrough came when she finally mastered her addition facts. This took sheer effort, but it paid off in spades. Once Tasha was freed from having to stop and work out basic problems like 7 + 8 every time they came up in a more complex problem, she could focus on the big picture and put her fine mind to work. Fluency with facts allowed her to put her mental energy into noticing patterns, making generalizations and conjectures, and tackling multistep word problems without getting bogged down. Even better, as a master of addition facts, Tasha began to see herself as someone who could do math. Confidence in her mastery of basic facts increased her engagement and willingness to take risks.

Vocabulary: From Reading to Math

Whatever the curriculum area, vocabulary plays a critical role in decoding, fluency, and comprehension. It is of no use to me that I can decode *perspicacity* if I don't know what it means; I can't explore the fascinating relationship between *area* and *perimeter* if I don't know what these words represent; and forget understanding the important difference between *similar* and *congruent* triangles!

Educators have long known that vocabulary development is clearly correlated with success in school, no matter what the curriculum area. In *Teaching Mathematics Vocabulary in Context*, Miki Murray cites several studies, dating back to 1944, that support this claim (2004, 4–5). If we want students to have the skills to decode and the ability to understand, we need to help them understand the terms they encounter. Precision and context count here: *similar* means one thing when you are looking at paintings and another when you are considering geometric shapes. Students must know the socially agreed upon meanings of words.

Vocabulary and Reading

In literacy, we have come a long way from simply looking words up in a dictionary. Educators like Isabel Beck, Heidi Hayes Jacobs, Diane Snowball, and Faye Bolton have advanced strategies for developing vocabulary that go well beyond rote memorization. Kate Kinsella and Kevin Feldman describe four components of "robust" vocabulary instruction in *Narrowing the Language Gap: The Case for Explicit Vocabulary Instruction* (2005): wide reading, explicit teaching of individual words, more general word-learning strategies, and student awareness of language.

Snowball and Bolton have written about ways to develop general word-learning strategies (1999). For example, they encourage teachers to have students learn the meanings of common derivatives and make lists of words that include them. For example, the prefix *tri-* conveys something about three and helps form such words as *tricycle, tripod, triplets, triple, triceratops,* and of course *triangle.* Not only do these explorations help students spell conventionally, but they also help them expand their vocabulary and give them tools for considering the meanings of unfamiliar words.

Bringing Words to Life: Robust Vocabulary Instruction (Beck, McKeown, and Kucan 2002) presents a structure for planning explicit instruction of important vocabulary. To help teachers choose appropriate words for study, the authors divided words into three tiers:

◆ Tier 1 words are those basic words we use regularly and that we generally learn without instruction—*girl, school, number, book, pencil.*

◆ Tier 2 words are "high frequency words for mature language users—*coincidence, absurd, industrious*" (16).

◆ Tier 3 words are domain specific and not otherwise frequently seen—*perpendicular, serf, estuary.*

Note: These tiers are not rigidly defined; a word may be more commonly known in some communities than in others.

This analysis helps teachers choose which words to investigate. While students need to know words from all three tiers to be successful readers and writers, in literacy it makes good sense to focus on developing students' Tier 2 vocabulary. Because words in this tier occur so often, the more students know these sophisticated high-frequency words, the better access they will have to increasingly challenging material. Tier 3 words are best explored in detail in the appropriate content area (*metamorphosis* in science, for example, or *immigrate* in social studies). These words can usually be explained briefly for the purposes of reading.

Vocabulary and Mathematics

The approaches for teaching vocabulary in literacy outlined previously are useful for thinking about the way we teach mathematics vocabulary. First, consider how examining the role of prefixes and suffixes in mathematics vocabulary helps students' comprehension. My fourth and fifth graders found that knowing that *oct-* means "eight" and *-gon* means "having a certain number of angles" helped them understand the meaning of the word *octagon* (as well as *octopus* and *hexagon*). This kind of word study is identical to the word study done in literacy. Individual word study, however, differs.

While in literacy students may be focusing on Tier 2 words, in mathematics most of the individual vocabulary words students are learning fall in Tier 3. *Perimeter, trapezoid,* and *factor* are words with specific meanings that belong to the world of mathematics. These are best learned as the student is learning the concepts they represent. Interestingly, many Tier 1 words—like *multiply, odd, face,* and *half*—may be considered Tier 3 words when students encounter them in the context of mathematics, as they have mathematical meanings that are quite different from their common ones. It is important to be explicit about this in our teaching of math.

When I told my fourth graders we were going to be exploring fractions, they had a lot to share from their experiences as third graders and life in general. "It's like halves and fourths and stuff," Camille began.

"Yeah, and my brother always gets the bigger half," added Luca. Everyone laughed.

"That's interesting," I said. "I've heard that a lot—the bigger half— but is it really possible? Could Luca's brother get the bigger half?"

I enjoy watching students when I open a discussion like this. Some kids shot up their hands so confidently that I was relieved to see their shoulders were still attached. Other kids looked uneasy—they'd certainly thought they'd been cheated out of the bigger half before—but yeah, something wasn't right. And yet others were so stone-faced I wasn't sure they had heard anything—which, in fact, they might not have. I repeated the question, and the conversation warmed up.

"Well, a half means something is cut in half. So it's equal. Or it should be," Jacob tried. Jacob had one of those seriously confident hands. Jacob was a great mathematical thinker, but like many kids, it was hard for him to put thoughts into words.

"Right," added Sara. "A half is one of two parts. *Equal* parts. Like, they should be exactly the same, or they aren't really halves."

Fiona raised her hand—unusual—and I called on her. "If the pieces aren't equal, then they are just pieces. Two pieces. So Luca's brother gets the bigger piece, not the bigger half."

I nodded. Still waters run deep!

Not favoring the possibility of being wrong, Luca mumbled, "It was just a joke. Besides, I like the way 'the bigger half' sounds better."

Here was my opportunity. "I agree, Luca. It has a good ring to it. It's just important to know that in math, words have really specific meanings, and in this case, what Sara, Jacob, and Fiona were saying is accurate. 'The Bigger Half' would make a great story title, though."

Luca smiled. It was a pretty good bet that it would, too.

These fourth graders were ready to learn that *half* had its colloquial usage *and* its mathematical meaning, and that each had its time and place. It is critical that students learn math vocabulary only *after* they understand the concepts underlying them. Only then can they define these words in language that makes sense to them and that they can refer back to. After our conversation about Luca's brother's bigger half, my class could write a definition of *half*—and I could expect to see them beginning to use the word appropriately.

The Whole Picture

Decoding, fluency, and vocabulary are all essential to success in literacy and mathematics. But they are not sufficient. We can try to tease apart the complementary skills of decoding and comprehending, but in the end they are inseparable. Whether the activity is reading or mathematics, to decode without understanding is boring, frustrating, and even, in a sense, dangerous. A child who grows accustomed to reading or doing mathematics without getting it is likely to lose interest in reading or doing mathematics. On the other hand, to understand without skill in decoding is also frustrating and likely to result in disenchanted learners. It is inappropriate to make meaning without making use of the author's words, and we simply cannot explore the fascinating realm of mathematics if we don't have access to the symbols representing the ideas. Comprehension, in the end, is our goal—no matter what the curriculum area.

FROM READING TO MATH TO YOUR CLASSROOM

1. *What do you think it means to be fluent in math? What signs of fluency can you look for in students?*

2. *What math contexts are you already providing students? What new ones can you add to your classroom?*

3. *What are the important Tier 3 words for the unit you're currently teaching? How can you help students learn this vocabulary?*

Teaching Comprehension

Does this describe you? If you have a student who is struggling to connect with his reading, you have a diverse collection of strategies you can draw from to help him engage with the text and monitor his comprehension, but when you have a student who isn't connecting with a math problem, you're not sure how to help her dive in. Good news! You already know a variety of ways to help that math learner comprehend her work.

Many years ago on a long car trip I volunteered to read aloud to my husband. As usual, Ken was reading two books at the time: *Iconology: Image, Text, Ideology*, a slim volume by W. J. T. Mitchell (1986), and *The Making of the Atomic Bomb*, the Pulitzer prize–winning nonfiction account of the Manhattan Project by Richard Rhodes (1995). I started with *Iconology*. As a former actress and teacher in training, I was comfortable cold reading—that is, reading an unfamiliar text aloud with expression. I opened the book to Ken's place marker and started to read. The text was well written, and I knew every word; in fact, with the exception of the title, I didn't encounter one unfamiliar word. Still, as I read, I became increasingly bored, confused, and even angry—I didn't *understand* a single thing I was reading. I made it sound like I did, and Ken was enjoying himself plenty. Eventually I confessed. *Iconology* was simply beyond my grasp—too advanced of a text on a topic unfamiliar to me. We switched to *The Making of the Atomic Bomb*. Ah, now that was the

29

ticket. Don't get me wrong—I stumbled over some of the scholarly names and scientific terms, but the story itself was completely absorbing. As Ken continued driving down the New Jersey Turnpike, the horror of Rhodes's description of the bombing of Nagasaki took over. I have never forgotten it.

Every teacher has encountered the child who decodes but draws no meaning—and little pleasure—from reading. Struggling through *Iconology*, though the words flowed freely, I gained little meaning and no pleasure. Decoding is a necessary component to reading, but it is certainly not everything.

In *Schools That Work: Where All Children Read and Write*, Richard Allington and Patricia Cunningham write, "Reading or writing without thinking would be senseless" (2006, 42). After all, the many functions of reading are all sense making—communicating, reflecting, reasoning, reminding, alarming, informing, recording, and so on. Either in our own reading or while observing students, we have all encountered the disquieting results of decoding without understanding, an activity that is at once boring and unnerving. Reading should be an engaging affair, whether it is purely business, deeply personal, or primarily aesthetic. It makes little sense, then, that in past decades so little elementary literacy instruction addressed the central issue of comprehension, focusing instead on the skills of decoding, spelling, grammar, and handwriting. Traditionally, comprehension instruction took the form of questions for the reader to answer—mostly literal ones relying on recall over reasoning. If such questions could be satisfactorily answered, comprehension was assumed.

Reading Comprehension: Understanding What Readers Do to Comprehend Texts

Fortunately, over the past couple of decades there has been a surge in interest in the teaching of reading comprehension. Research into the specific mental processes involved in understanding written text has inspired work by such educators as Ellin Keene and Susan Zimmermann (*Mosaic of Thought* 1997), Stephanie Harvey and Anne Goudvis (*Strategies That Work* 2000), and Diane Snowball (the CD-ROM course *Teaching Comprehension*). Though the authors approach the topics in their own ways, the same essential strategies turn up again and again: tapping prior knowledge, questioning, inferring, visualizing, summarizing, synthesizing, and monitoring and repairing understanding:

Seven Comprehension Strategies

1. tapping prior knowledge (or making connections)
2. questioning
3. inferring
4. visualizing
5. summarizing
6. synthesizing
7. monitoring and repairing understanding

These strategies are habits of mind, and they're some of the same strategies learners use to make sense of math. Before looking at how we use these comprehension strategies in the math classroom, let's look at a brief definition of each one as it works in reading.

Tapping Prior Knowledge
Readers make use of prior knowledge to understand new texts. Personal experience, background knowledge, and previous reading experiences all support readers in making sense of reading. Educators may refer to this mental process as *activating prior knowledge* (Snowball) or *making connections* (Keene and Harvey). Readers use prior knowledge to make predictions as they read. Accurate or not, predictions pull readers through a text and encourage the forming and reforming of theories about a text's meaning. In reading, we encourage students to make three kinds of connections: text-to-self, text-to-text, and text-to-world.

Questioning
Readers ask questions as they read. Harvey and Goudvis (2000) borrow the phrase "puzzle drive" from physicist Richard Feynman to describe the power of questions to motivate learners. Readers may ask questions that are literal and specific ("How long is the fruit bat's gestation?" or "How can Charlotte save a pig's life?") or questions that

draw in the reader through the plot ("How is Percy going to get out of this mess?" or "Will Beth die?"). Readers pose questions to identify with their reading ("What would I do?"), challenge the author's ideas ("How in the world are you going to defend that?"), or clarify confusion ("What happened? Who stole the red sweater?"). Questioning is often a barely conscious but constant reading activity; it wires us to the texts we read.

Inferring and Visualizing

Readers make inferences both while reading and while reflecting on their reading. Inferring is in fact a life skill; we are taught to use it through our daily interactions with other people. As children we learn to observe the faces of the people around us to discern the best time to ask for a treat or when it's best to leave someone alone. The inferring readers do is a complex skill. Reading requires that we go beyond the literal—considering both what we know and clues from the text—so we can capture mood, follow themes, and understand and evaluate ideas. Visualizing (and other sensory imaging) is a strategy that not only enhances the quality of the reading experience—"hearing" Chester Cricket's symphonies or "seeing" the lush and beautiful forests of Rivendell—but also helps readers infer meaning that is not explicitly stated. For example, the description of an ominously gloomy house clues us into danger, though such isn't mentioned directly. When we read that Mother says something curtly with her eyes averted, we envision her being unhappy. Visualizing also helps readers monitor their comprehension; if we can't see all elements of a setting or situation in our mind's eye ("How did Harry get out of that locked room?"), we get a powerful clue that we missed something in the text and that we might want to reread to straighten things out.

Summarizing

Proficient readers distinguish what is most important to the theme, plot, or thesis of the texts they read from less essential details. This is true for both fiction, in which some details create mood and others drive plot, and nonfiction, in which some pieces of information carry more importance than others (it is more important to know that the tiger is a carnivore, for example, than that he is a swimmer). The skill of determining importance does not come easily or automatically to most readers. Readers must learn to distinguish the difference between what is important in the context of the text and what is personally important to the reader. It may be important to the reader, for example, that she shares a birthday with the runner Wilma Rudolph, but it is not important overall to the text of Rudolph's biography.

Synthesizing

In this complex comprehension strategy, readers use the text they are reading to go beyond the reading experience. Like inferring, synthesizing requires readers to consider both what they know and what they are reading, but in this case the object is to emerge with an entirely new idea or degree of understanding. Children reading one creation myth after another add new information onto old and build an understanding of this genre beyond what any one story contains. The same process occurs when students read several books on dinosaurs: each source contributes new pieces of information that the reader then adds to his bank of understanding. Synthesizing requires the fluid use of other reading strategies. In many respects, synthesizing is the goal of reading. We read to extend our understanding of ourselves and the world.

Monitoring and Repairing Understanding

Finally, readers must pay attention to the quality of their understanding. When understanding fails, readers need to take action. They may reread a confusing passage, seek clarification from another source, or select another text altogether. Again, this can be a difficult skill to acquire. Young readers in particular don't necessarily know what good comprehension feels like, especially when their primary focus is decoding. They need to learn that good comprehension is "like watching TV," as fourth-grade Lamar exclaimed.

Teaching comprehension is challenging. Though these strategies are distinct, it is artificial to isolate them. Proficient readers simultaneously visualize a scene while they are drawing on prior knowledge and posing questions. Therefore, teachers must take care not to oversimplify the strategies when we introduce them and should avoid teaching strict procedures for questioning, making connections, visualizing, and so on. Rather, we serve readers best by introducing them to the way our own minds work, revealing and reflecting on our own comprehension processes, and teaching children to practice and reflect on theirs.

In order to help my students acquire these sophisticated habits of mind, I follow four steps:

Four Steps to Teaching Comprehension

1. *Teacher modeling:* In this stage I describe a comprehension strategy and model its use, explaining aloud what I am thinking as I do so.

2. *Guided practice:* My students then practice the strategy with my support. This may take place in a whole group, in small groups, or one-on-one. I encourage them to think aloud so I can give them immediate feedback.

3. *Independent practice:* Students then begin using the new comprehension strategy in their independent reading. Consciously applying the strategy, they jot down notes in the margins, mark pages with sticky notes, or engage in conversations with reading partners.

4. *Incorporation into real reading situations:* Finally, students make use of reading strategies, without my support, in a range of reading situations. If all has gone well, this use is automatic and spontaneous, responsive to the particular reading situation. To assess their comprehension work, I stay in touch with students through written responses, one-on-one conversations, and the monitoring of book clubs or reading partnerships.

Teaching Math Comprehension Using Reading Comprehension Strategies

As in reading, comprehension is the ultimate goal of mathematics. And as in reading, teachers can no longer rest on the assumption that when a mathematical skill is mastered, understanding will naturally follow. Instead, we need to teach students what math comprehension means—what it feels like to really understand the math they do—and how they can develop it.

It makes sense to borrow the language of reading comprehension when teaching math. We want students to apply the same sophisticated habits of mind they use as readers when they think about math. In the following pages, the mental strategies used for reading comprehension are applied to the world of math. It is my hope that such applications help us improve our teaching for math comprehension.

Tapping Prior Knowledge (Making Connections) in Mathematics

There is nothing more dispiriting to a math teacher than to see students utterly disengaged with math. Unfortunately, this often happens when students are moved too quickly into procedures, before they understand the actual function of the numbers and symbols. Once, when I visited a fifth-grade math class in a different school. I spent time with an eleven-year-old slogging through a list of percent problems. Her task was to calculate a 25 percent discount on a number of items desirable to kids her age. Alicia was a discounting machine, capably calculating the sales prices but otherwise completely unconnected to the work. "Twenty-five percent off!" I interjected. "That's pretty good." Alicia shrugged. I tried to tap into something that might interest her: Would she buy one of the items at that sale price? What kind of a discount would tempt her? Could she play a little with fractional equivalents to figure sales prices in her head? After all, she'd be unlikely to shop with paper and pencil in hand. My questions did nothing for her: Alicia could tell me an answer, but she could say little else. In other words, she was lacking comprehension of the task. Alicia was not drawing on her prior knowledge (of fractions or other percents) or her experiences as a consumer to think deeply about the math she was doing.

One of mathematics' special qualities is its exquisite connectedness to real life. I want my students to make use of math beyond the classroom. In many classrooms, however, math is often a decidedly disconnected discipline. There is a long tradition in emphasizing procedural, abstract paths to mathematical understanding, and although by and large such procedures are efficient and accurate, to be used wisely they require an aware and reasoning mind. What is missing in many classrooms are connections to the physical and social world. While there is a nod to the interconnectedness of mathematical concepts, it is mostly in careful sequencing of topics (fractions followed by decimals then percents, or addition then subtraction).

Even word problems, which ask students to apply the math they are learning to real-life situations, are often taught in a disconnected way: we coach students to look for keywords to figure out which operation to choose. For example, *altogether* means to add while *how many more* means to subtract. Of course, it is possible to find situations where that will not work (*Mary and Frank each brought 12 cupcakes to the party. When the party was over there were 3 left. How many were eaten altogether?*), and real-life situations rarely come with keywords. On the other hand, making connections to past experiences is a very effective mathematical habit of mind; if you can reason about Mary and Frank's cupcakes, you will not be tripped up by the unorthodox use of the word *altogether*. By making connections, students are empowered to understand the math they are doing.

As previously stated, we encourage readers to make three kinds of connections: text-to-self, text-to-text, and text-to-world. In the world of mathematics, students enhance understanding and build mathematical knowledge by making math-to-self connections, math-to-math connections, and math-to-world connections.

Math-to-Self Connections
Students making math-to-self connections relate unfamiliar mathematical material to personal experiences. Personal experiences help them think about how the math might work and whether answers make sense.

When my fifth graders where learning division with double-digit divisors, I presented them with a (disappointingly imaginary) scenario: An anonymous donor had given her collection of 3,293 nickels to our class of thirty-one students on the condition that each child get the same number of nickels. In addition, the technophobic donor forbade the use of computers or calculators. The students' mission? To determine how many nickels each would receive (and, subsequently, how much money that was and what they planned to buy—including tax!).

The problem itself was messy, but the situation—while implausible—was imaginable, even enticing. While kids may say, "I can't figure out three thousand two hundred ninety-three divided by thirty-one," they are unlikely to say, "If this really happened, I'd give the money back." Every child has had the experience of sharing things, sometimes among groups and in large quantities (a bag of M&Ms, for example). By connecting this scenario with their experiences, children had a way in, a starting point for solving a challenging arithmetic problem. My students drew from their personal experiences to complete the task. They soon realized that counting out and sharing the nickels one by one was extremely impractical, and they began to seek ways to share out larger numbers at a time. Every child was able to figure out that the fair share was 106 nickels, with 7 nickels left over. That meant they each would get $5.30, and they quickly started planning ways to spend it.

Interestingly, this same problem was declared impossible by one student's father because the answer involved a remainder. The father simply did not know how to deal with a remainder in a situation demanding equal distribution. In fact, remainders, which occur more often than not in real-world division situations, are often best understood by drawing on connections. Numbers, chocolate bars, nickels, and balloons will all need to be dealt with differently according to their unique qualities.

Math-to-Math Connections
Students benefit from the use of the interconnectedness of mathematical concepts to learn new material. For example, traditionally fractions, decimals, and percents are taught separately and sequentially; students are expected to master fraction concepts and operations with fractions before proceeding to tackle decimals and percents. However, in TERC's *Investigations in Number, Data, Space* unit *Name That Portion* (Akers et al. 1998), the three topics overlap; fifth-grade students gain valuable insight into all three and have abundant opportunities to relate the topics. In one activity, students find percent equivalents for fractions using familiar fraction-percent equivalents as places to start ($\frac{1}{2}$ = 50% and $\frac{3}{3}$ = 100%). This powerful exercise builds students' understanding of the magnitude of fractions and percents and supports the use of effective mental math strategies for finding equivalence (if $\frac{1}{4}$ equals 25%, and $\frac{1}{8}$ is half of $\frac{1}{4}$, then the percent equivalent to $\frac{1}{8}$ is half of 25%, or 12.5%).

While there is an equally effective procedural approach to finding percent equivalents to fractions, without a sound understanding of the connectedness of these two mathematical concepts, many students find the procedure difficult to recall and execute. By contrast, my fifth-grade students found this activity stimulating and engaging—or in their words, "cool"—and they were able to use what they learned to mentally compare the fractions three-eighths and two-fifths. This math-to-math connection helped them develop comprehension of a potentially puzzling set of numbers (fractions) and a challenging mathematical concept (percents).

Math-to-World Connections

By connecting new concepts to what they know about the world, students deepen their understanding of mathematics. For example, third graders studying measurement benefit from relating real-world containers to abstract units of measurement. Though you can tell students how many ounces are in a cup, how many cups are in a pint, how many pints in a quart, and how many quarts in a gallon, they are more likely to understand these relationships (and remember them) by comparing a standard school-issue carton of milk (1 cup) with pint, quart, half-gallon, and gallon containers of milk. By looking at, holding, and pouring with these different everyday containers, students make tactile and visual connections between familiar real-world objects and abstract information. While it will be necessary for them to learn the name of each container's volume, making this math-to-world connection gives students a concrete reference point that they can recall at any time from memory.

Questioning in Mathematics

Questions are at the heart of learning. Our need to question is what drives human beings to new, deeper, more accurate understandings as well as new fields of study; before the age of quantum physics, no one knew to ask, "What is dark matter?"

Students benefit from direct and explicit instruction in how to use questioning as a math comprehension strategy. However, explicit teaching of questioning as a math comprehension strategy is not sufficient to help students become questioners by habit. The asking of good questions must be a part of the culture of the classroom. Teachers often get into a questioning rut, posing one-answer, read-my-mind sorts of questions: "What is a square number?" "How many sides does a rhombus have?" While there will always be a place for these kinds of questions, they do ask very little of a learner, sometimes requiring no thinking beyond recall.

In *Good Questions for Math Teaching: Why Ask Them and What to Ask*, Lainie Schuster and Nancy Canavan Anderson describe good questions as "open-ended, whether in answer or approach" (2005, 3). In a classroom where questioning is valued, you should model types of questions that push learners beyond one answer in their mathematical thinking: "Is there a pattern here?" "Will this always work?" "Why does this work?" These are the kinds of questions that encourage learners to explore new territory.

Another way for teachers to learn how to ask good questions is to think about how we listen. Early childhood teacher Ann Carlyle said, "I try never to ask children a question that I know the answer to." As she described it, asking such questions limited her listening. When you ask, "What is seven plus seven?" you are listening for fourteen. In contrast, when you ask, "How did you solve seven plus seven?" you have no idea what a child is going to say, and hence you must listen more closely.

By modeling good questioning, we teach children the kinds of thinking we value. When we respond to students who ask, "Is this right?" with our own question, "What do you think?" we are communicating our belief that the quality of their thinking is more important than the answer alone.

While students benefit from being taught a general questioning habit of mind, there are types of questions that specifically help students understand math. These question types fall into four categories:

Four Types of Math Questions

questions that help students get started
questions that help students get unstuck
questions that help students check work
questions that help students go deeper

Getting Started

Questioning moves readers forward. When readers pick up a book, they pose a number of questions to themselves: "What will this be about? Will I like it as much as the author's other books? Will it be too hard or too easy for me?" As they delve into the first pages, new questions move them along: "Where is this taking place? Who is the main character? Is this happening now, or long ago?" In finding answers to these initial, stage-setting questions, readers fully immerse themselves in the worlds of their books.

Questions serve a similar purpose in mathematics. Faced with a new problem, activity, or game, young learners often find themselves at a loss. Whether they are beginning work on an investigation of number patterns, using geoboards to explore common fractions, or solving a story problem, despite the clearest of instructions, students often do not know where to start.

When students come to me with their getting-started questions ("What do I do?"), I respond with a compliment ("I'm glad you asked!") and then pose questions of my own:

◆ "Do you remember what I said? If not, is there someone at your table you can ask? Is there somewhere you can look?" I want to foster responsibility and independence.

◆ "Do you have the materials you need? Look around—what are other kids using?" Sometimes students can be quite passive in the classroom. Again, I want to encourage their active responsibility in their own work.

◆ "What's the very first thing you are going to do? And then what?" If the child can answer the first question, the answer to the second is often "Oh! I get it." If not, I know I have reteaching to do.

Eventually I return the questions to the students: "Have you asked yourself . . . what I told you to do today? what materials you need? how you plan to get started?"

Learning how to ask themselves getting-started questions is particularly helpful for students who approach math with trepidation. These learners are often caught staring blankly at their work. They need explicit instruction on how to crack open a math problem so they can make use of what they do know. Questioning themselves and others helps them get started.

Getting Unstuck

Questions help readers navigate confusing parts of their books. When understanding breaks down, it is critical for readers to notice their confusion and to seek clarification: "Wait a minute—what happened to the dog?" "Why did they leave in the middle of the show?" "Whoa—what does *spontaneously combusted* mean?" Readers learn to respond to such questions in a variety of ways: turning to a more experienced reader for definitions, rereading, examining illustrations, or looking at another text for additional information.

Getting-unstuck questions help students deal with the inevitable confusion they will experience while exploring mathematics. At some point a strategy will dead-end, or a pattern will start acting unpredictably. These are challenging moments; confusion is an uncomfortable sensation, and students often feel helpless in the grips of it. Though you will need to teach students how to pose getting-unstuck questions, doing so will help diagnose their roadblocks and point to a way to get back on track: "Where did my pattern stop working?" "If I can't find any more fourths this way, what other strategies can I try?" "Did I read the question right?" "Did I make any mistakes so far?" Such questions prompt learners to reread their work, looking for where math went awry or where confusion set in, seeking help from another person, or turning to another resource (a calculator, for example).

Checking Work

Students can make good use of questioning to evaluate the reason-ableness or accuracy of their work. Although learners typically turn to the teacher or another authority—such as the kid known to be good in math—to find out if they are right, the habit of questioning helps learners both verify their solutions on their own and deepen their understanding.

When students ask me, "Is this right?" my answer is "What do you think?" After all, the answer will be right on its own merits, not because I deem it right. If the math is not too hard, students should be able to determine if their solutions are accurate. They can do this by asking themselves a series of questions.

One of the most valuable questions students can ask is "Does my answer make sense?" This is a giant step away from "Is my answer right?" because it encourages students to look at the answer in con-text. Often students rely on a dependable procedure to determine the correctness of an answer—"the answer must be right because I subtracted the right way"—without considering the reasonableness of the solution. When we teach students to evaluate the reasonableness of their work (by considering the magnitude of the number and the context, for example), they can spot significant errors quickly (and are reminded again that we value reasonableness!).

Next, I want students to ask themselves, "How do I know it is right?" They may verify their work by checking it over, using a testing technique (e.g., adding to test the results of subtraction), or using an alternative method to solve the problem again, including such technology as a calculator. This is really valuable work. Students become both mathematically powerful and confident when they depend upon themselves to prove their work, instead of relying on the teacher as the arbiter of correctness.

Going Deeper

The power of questioning rests in its potential for leading learners into new territory. Neither reading nor the study of mathematics is a finite activity. When we are reading wide-awake, we are able to go well beyond the literal meaning of the text to challenge our own ideas, create new theories about the world, and gain deeply personal insights. We are often impelled to do this by raising and persistently pursuing questions: Why are humans so prone to do evil? What does it mean to be a friend? Where does a person draw the line between self-interest and the needs of the community? These are the kinds of questions that have no answer but drive us to learn and think all the same.

Elementary mathematics is the gateway to a limitless universe of questions. As much as we value a solid skill base and sound conceptual knowledge, it is at least as vital to help students develop open and questioning minds. We want students to be skilled problem solvers, and to that end they must learn to be astute questioners.

When my first class of fourth and fifth graders was engaged in a study of factors, they became curious about the number zero. They were discovering all sorts of interesting things about patterns in multiples, square numbers, primes, and even and odd numbers. Zero began to perplex them: What was it, anyway? Even or odd? This deeply provocative question (well, it was deeply provocative to them) took us on a bit of a detour from our focus on multiplication, but what a payoff! Together, we looked at zero through the lens of patterns, number theory, the history of mathematics, and contemporary understanding. It was a richly engaging mathematics adventure with lessons that ultimately went beyond understanding the nature of zero.

Inferring and Visualizing in Mathematics

In books as in life, meaning is often found beyond the immediate details. Visualizing (including other sensory images) is a way to enhance our ability to infer and monitor our understanding of meaning. When we succeed in building sensory images while reading Laura Ingalls Wilder's *The Long Winter* (1940), for example, we feel the horror of the bitter, cold, endless howling winds that the Ingalls family endures for seven dark months. We admire Laura's strength of character and meet the arrival of spring with relief and gratitude. Visualizing helps us monitor understanding, too. When we expect to make mental images and then have trouble building them, it's difficult for us to feel any connections. In such cases we've probably missed an important detail or two, or the book may be too hard—or maybe even badly written!

Visualizing in mathematics serves these same functions and more. Proficient math learners expect to have sensory connections to the math they are doing. Whether it is seeing a mental number line or grid, visualizing mental manipulation of numerals or shapes, or seeing story problems in context, sensory images deepen appreciation and comprehension *and* signal problems. Sensory images that are incomplete or don't make sense drive learners back to repair meaning.

Visualizing is also a math comprehension strategy that helps learners solve problems and deepen understanding. Because it is so important, teachers incorporate it into lesson design. However, even though we may talk explicitly about visualizing as a math comprehension strategy and offer guided practice to students ("What do you picture when I say triangle?" or "Try imagining the story problem; will Mary have more dinosaurs after Stewart leaves or fewer?"), students still need support on *how* to create appropriate images that they can recall later from memory (in many cases, learners do not yet have visual or sensory images for the material they are learning). By incorporating manipulative materials, drawings, and everyday objects into math lessons, teachers help students build a visual vocabulary for math concepts. Once students have used such real materials to solve problems and defend their solutions, the tools remain as mental images to draw on in the future.

The *Encyclopedia Britannica Online Encyclopedia* (n.d.) defines mathematics as the "science of structure, order, and relation that has evolved from elemental practices of counting, measuring, and describing the shapes of objects." In other words, mathematics is an outgrowth of the physical world. In many beautiful and intriguing ways, mathematical thinking has gone beyond the physical into the theoretical while retaining the logic of reality. Here on firm ground, we experience math throughout our daily lives. We draw on our experiences to create sensory images in three realms: number, shape, and measurement.

Visualizing and Numbers

Numbers are abstract. As adults, we know them so well it is easy to forget how much information is embedded in them and hard to remember all the work children need to do to become as comfortable as we are with them. (And, truth be told, a lot of us are friendly only with a small group of numbers. Some of us have resolved to never gain a comfortable familiarity with fractions, negative integers, or irrational numbers.)

Visualizing is a powerful strategy for thinking about numbers and number relationships. Learners can draw on both personal experiences and internalized visual models. For example, number lines help learners understand sequence and compute numbers. A physical or mental number line is very useful in solving the problem $102 - 4$ without resorting to pencil and paper. Number grids (a 10-by-10 grid with the numbers 1–100 or 0–99) can be used to explore patterns, develop place-value concepts, and compute numbers.

Place-value concepts are often very challenging to young children. We help them by providing visual models. On the first day of school, for example, I introduce second graders with a task they will continue all year long: counting and keeping track of the days of school. On day one, I place a sheet of white paper above the board and put a cup on the chalk tray. "Boys and girls," I say, "today is the first day of school. This year we are going to keep track of all the days we come to school. We are going to do it two ways.

"On this sheet of paper," I continue, pointing above the board, "we will write the number of days we have come to school. In addition, we will place a craft stick in this cup for each day we come to school."

Usually a brother or sister of a former second-grade student chimes in, excitedly claiming, "And on the hundredth day of school . . . we get to go ice-skating!"

"That's right," I affirm. After the excited hubbub dies down, we mark the first day of school together: I write a number *1* at the beginning of the sheet of paper and place a craft stick in the cup; the stick hits the bottom with a ceremonial thud. As promised, we do this every day. As the string of numbers grows longer and the cup fuller, the children explore the patterns they observe when they count by twos, fives, and tens. They also become aware of the cup reaching its capacity for sticks; at this point students begin bundling groups of ten sticks and placing them in a separate cup. This is one of many activities students engage in over the course of a year to build their understanding—through visual models—of the base ten number system.

Our youngest learners benefit from visual models as well. Kindergartners and first graders develop their understanding of small numbers by representing them with objects. Counting and arranging five tiles, for example, helps learners internalize the quantity five and the parts it is made of (such as 2 + 3 or 1 + 4). Fingers, an early favorite counting tool, also become internalized—when young students are asked to put their mental strategies for addition on paper, they often draw the imaginary fingers they have counted!

Learners also use visualizing to solve story problems. When I asked a class of fourth graders to figure out how many vans a class of twenty-seven would need to go on a field trip if each van held six kids, being good with numbers was not enough to solve this problem. Students crunching numbers came up with the answers 4 R3 and $4\frac{1}{2}$, neither of which tells how many vans would be needed. Students that drew or imagined the context were more likely to realize that the remainder of three really meant three kids who needed a van to go on the fied trip and come up with the correct answer of five vans. When the numbers were the same but the context was different (twenty-seven dollars between six babysitters, for example, or twenty-seven balloons between six partygoers), visualizing continued to be an extremely effective way to make sense of remainders and decide what to do with them.

Visualizing is also a powerful way to understand magnitude. Even adults have difficulty conceptualizing such numbers as a billion; visual representations help us get a sense of their magnitude. In *Exploring the Night Sky with Binoculars*, David Chandler (2005) uses grains of sand to create visual representations of large numbers: One thousand grains of sand in a single line would be about a yard long, a million grains of sand would form a square yard of sand one grain thick, and a cubic yard would contain about a *billion* grains of sand. Or, 1,000 seconds is about 17 minutes, 1,000,000 seconds is 13 days, and 1,000,000,000 seconds is 31 years. These visual comparisons help put these tremendously large numbers in perspective!

Visualizing and Shapes

Geometry is an area of mathematics that is decidedly visual. Too often, however, students rush from physical representations of geometric concepts to abstract definitions and formulas. When the mental link between the concrete and abstract is weak, many learners find it difficult to retain understanding of concepts such as pi or formulas such as $A = lw$.

Manipulatives help learners represent ideas visually. Students can build the concept of symmetry by folding paper shapes or creating symmetrical designs with blocks. The physical act of making symmetrical images helps learners create a mental image to refer to in the future.

Young learners develop and extend basic concepts of geometry, such as the qualities of a triangle, both by identifying shapes in the environment and by making shapes out of physical materials. When students create a variety of triangles from different lengths of straws, they move beyond a common early misconception that triangles are all equilateral. Interacting with real objects is extremely powerful; although children can be told that triangles are shapes with three sides and shown examples of different triangles, if they make the triangles themselves, their mental links to the concept are much stronger.

A group of first graders I was teaching had a lively discussion about whether a square resting on one corner was really a diamond. The convincing argument was made by one child who took a paper square and dramatically flapped it around, asking his classmates, "It's a square, right?" The child then positioned the paper on its corner and froze in midair. Slyly smiling, he stated, "It's still a square."

Visualizing and Measurements

In *About Teaching Mathematics*, Marilyn Burns wrote that measurement involves the comparison "between what is being measured and some suitable standard of measure" (2007, 70). Young children will directly compare objects with themselves to determine their size. Their measurement technique makes obvious sense to them: they can see which is bigger. As we ask students to use increasingly abstract tools for comparison, we must help them use sensory images to make sense of them. For example, third graders who mess around with milk cartons have powerful mental images to draw on when thinking about liquid measurement.

There are aspects of measurement that cannot be constructed, or figured out, no matter how clever the student or how engaging the activity. We all need to be told the names for units of measurement and then shown what they represent. The extensive vocabulary involved in measurement requires an enormous amount of remembering, and it is much easier for students to remember measurement terms when they can picture them. Having handled hundreds of sticky notes, I can easily visualize 3 inches, for example, and having bought hundreds (thousands!) of pounds of butter, I have a strong sensory memory of a pound.

In the classroom, using common manipulatives like color tiles helps students create a visual representation of an inch (or square inch, as needed). Children who work with Cuisinaire rods, which are measured in centimeter increments, can visualize a centimeter. Children can also create sensory images to think about weight: for example, a slice of bread and a penny each weigh about 1 ounce. Such mental images, or sensory memories, are useful in remembering measurement terms and creating a frame of reference for them: not only can we mentally compare, but we can make decisions about what standard of measurement is suitable in a given situation.

Summarizing and Synthesizing in Mathematics

Proficient readers are continually and unconsciously summarizing as they read. As they are carried along by the language and action of a text, they are also discriminating between what mostly colors their appreciation and what definitely needs to be kept in mind to continue making sense of the plot. All writing includes both essential and nonessential details. The color of Lucy's hair in *The Lion, the Witch and the Wardrobe* (Lewis 1950) is not important to the plot, but the fact that it is winter in Narnia is very important. Proficient readers know how to take note of interesting but nonessential details without dwelling on them and to hold onto the more important threads as they work their way through a story. Nonfiction is no different: the pertinent information needs to be sifted from descriptive details.

Once readers have extracted the essential understandings of a text, they must make it work for them, synthesizing new thoughts with previously held ideas and emerging with improved understanding. Synthesizing is a complex and sophisticated process. Readers must also summarize what is important about their reflections, reactions, and opinions, and be prepared to be changed by the act of reading. Sometimes we get more evidence for existing ideas; at other times new information suggests our ideas need revising. In synthesizing, readers use a number of comprehension strategies at once: they are drawing on prior knowledge, thinking about their connections, reflecting on their questions, evoking sensory images, and considering these in context of the most important aspects of the text. The comprehension represented by synthesizing is a key goal of reading.

Summarizing and synthesizing are critical math comprehension strategies as well. In mathematics, students must distill important ideas and synthesize them with previously acquired knowledge. For example, during a fourth-grade study of the array model of multiplication, I asked students to find all possible rectangular arrays for the numbers 9, 12, 13, 16, and 24 using color tiles. To help students make sense of the problem, I gave them a compelling context devised by Marilyn Burns: the arrays would be used to design candy boxes (a math-to-world connection).

In working on this problem, students made use of several math comprehension strategies:

◆ *Making math-to-self connections:* Students related the array model to their own previous experiences with candy.

◆ *Making math-to-math connections:* Students used previous knowledge of factor pairs to construct possible arrays.

◆ *Questioning:* Students asked questions: "What if I try one across first, then try two, then three, and so on?" Or "Have I found them all? How can I be sure?" Or "Why do only some make squares?"

◆ *Visualizing:* Students made use of visual representations: "Rectangles can be short and fat or long and skinny; have we tried them all?"

◆ *Summarizing:* Students distinguished important findings from those that were interesting but irrelevant. For example, it is important mathematically and relevant to this problem that all numbers have arrays that are one tile wide. It is interesting but irrelevant that they can be built with an alternating, checkerboard pattern.

Following their explorations, students went on to synthesize information. These are some of the generalizations they made:

Examples of Synthesizing Information in Math

All the even numbers had arrays that were two tiles across.
All numbers have an array that is one tile across.
The number thirteen could make only one array.
The two square numbers actually make square arrays!
The number of arrays is the same as the number of factor pairs.

By drawing conclusions from this activity, students expanded their understanding of multiplication. They also had the opportunity to form questions that advanced their thinking: "What other numbers can be made with only one array, like thirteen?" "What other numbers make squares? Why?" and "Which number makes the most arrays?"

Monitoring and Repairing Understanding in Mathematics

Whether they are reading or doing mathematics, students need to expect that what they are doing makes sense—and take action if it doesn't. For proficient learners, part of the mind is always paying attention to the overall sense of the work. That is not to say that we expect all our work to be crystal clear; readers do encounter and tolerate some ambiguity and mystery as they read, as do people engaged in rich and complex math problems. But if there is not a sense that we are on the right track and that clarity is around the corner, we must take some action.

To this end, learners need to know what good math comprehension feels like. Just as readers come to understand that good reading comprehension has certain qualities—a sense of immediacy, for example, or clear imagery, or even a feeling of empathy—students should come to have similar expectations about the math they are doing. Though we may be journeying into new territory, we have mental tools to make sense of what we are encountering.

Not surprisingly, the most powerful strategy teachers have is to model their own expectation that math will make sense. This is no small task. Many of us are not entirely comfortable with the mathematics we teach, and we may have arrived at superficial comprehension ourselves. In my experience, it can feel extremely uncomfortable as a teacher to discover that you don't fully understand the math you are teaching your fourth graders. On the flip side, it is extremely liberating, and enormously helpful, to say, "I don't know. Let's find out together."

The Whole Picture

Comprehension is not an absolute. Depending on our students' ages, good math comprehension ranges from being able to relate one-half to its decimal and percent equivalents and visualize it in a number of contexts to being able to tell whether your kindergarten buddy got "the bigger half." All students, whether reading or doing mathematics, are somewhere on the comprehension continuum. Our job as teachers is to help them value the meaning they are making and thirst for more. We can do that only when we value the rich meaning of mathematics ourselves—and have patience and tolerance to see how we can also thirst for more.

FROM READING TO MATH TO YOUR CLASSROOM

1. *Think of a math unit you teach. How could you help students use the comprehension strategies discussed in this chapter to learn the content of that unit?*

2. *How will you know if students are making meaning in math? What can you do if they are not making meaning?*

3. *What other questions could you ask students in math to help them get started, get unstuck, check their work, or go deeper?*

4. *How can you rephrase questions you commonly ask so that you don't know the answers before asking the questions?*

5. *How will you know when students are comprehending math? What signs will you look for?*

Organizing the Classroom

During math time, does your classroom look and feel like a different place than during literacy time? For example, are students working independently instead of collaboratively? Does it feel like teaching is a one-way process, with information moving from you to the class, rather than a back-and-forth process, with teaching and learning flowing between you and the students and from student to student? What would happen if you structured your math time like your literacy time?

I n *Learning to Read: Lessons from Exemplary First-Grade Classrooms*, literacy educator Michael Pressley and his colleagues (2001) depart from the usual debate—What is the one best way to teach reading?—to examine what the most successful classrooms across the country actually have in common. The authors defined a classroom as successful by looking at standardized test scores, the difficulty of books students were reading by the year's end, and the quality of student writing. The exemplary classrooms differed from each other in many respects: some were in rural areas, others urban; some had student populations in the hundreds, others in the thousands; class sizes were rarely the same; and, last but not least, materials covered the whole range of shapes, sizes, and forms. As it turns out, what made a classroom successful was a variety of factors, none of which could be deemed as the all-in-one way.

Nevertheless, the team of educators found the classrooms to have the following common attributes:

◆ Skills are explicitly taught throughout the day through dozens of brief minilessons, most of which take place as teachers identify students' needs.

◆ Literature is emphasized. Successful classrooms tend to have large libraries with a wide variety of high-quality children's trade books. Teachers' instruction makes optimal use of these materials.

◆ Teachers and students engage frequently in reading of all kinds. Writing is a daily activity.

◆ Teachers have high, realistic expectations for their students. Teachers are skilled in matching students with tasks that challenge but don't frustrate.

◆ Students are encouraged to self-regulate, and teachers explicitly teach strategies for self-regulation (an example is appropriate book choice).

◆ Literacy activities are integrated throughout the curriculum, so students make use of the reading and writing skills they are learning all day long. This includes vocabulary development and the use of thematic units.

◆ In the most successful classrooms, the learning environment is strikingly warm and caring. Teachers continually encourage cooperative learning and risk taking.

◆ Classroom management is seamless:
  • Teachers communicate clear rules, expectations, and effective routines.
  • Plans are thorough but open to change and adapted as needed to respond to students.
  • Tasks are academically rich.

- Teachers select grouping structures according to the specifics of lessons and the needs of the students. Classrooms are organized to accommodate a variety of grouping structures.
- Homework is purposeful, often serving multiple goals.
- Discipline issues are dealt with quickly, and students spend most of the school day on task.
- Appropriate resources are directed to students with special needs and, where possible, students receive additional support in the classroom.

It is not hard to see why these attributes foster success in learning. In a successful classroom, students are motivated, orderly, and appropriately challenged. Teachers are warm, direct, and focused on student needs. The environment is safe, noncompetitive, and designed for student independence. And curriculum is rigorous and responsive. More teachers are striving to make these commonalities happen in their literacy teaching.

However, a strange phenomenon happens when we turn to mathematics. Teachers who readily agree with the factors for successful literacy instruction often turn their classrooms into very different places when math time rolls around. Let's revisit the attributes of successful classrooms, now in terms of mathematics:

◆ Instead of teaching many minilessons throughout the day as needs arise, teachers teach one lesson at one time: math time. The lesson is generally determined by the pacing calendar instead of students' needs or interests.

◆ There is little time to explore mathematics that emerges throughout the day, and teachers get little support for learning how to deal with those teachable math moments.

◆ The math being taught comes from a set curriculum. Teachers think in terms of teaching *Brand X math* instead of teaching math *using Brand X and other high-quality materials.*

◆ While teachers are becoming increasingly skillful at matching students with *just-right* books—that is, books right at students' independent reading level—math is still by and large a one-size-fits-all affair. All students are expected to complete the same assignment; as a result, teachers struggle to support students who find the work too hard and simultaneously struggle to challenge students who find the work too easy.

◆ Students have little opportunity to self-regulate. Materials are distributed as needed for specific lessons, instead of being seen as learning tools that are accessible at all times. There is little or no choice of activities; even methods are prescribed. Correctness is usually determined by the teacher, who responds to right answers with prompts like "Good" or "Excellent!" and wrong answers with "No" or "Try again."

◆ Though teachers may be warm and caring, when math time comes, they are reluctant to allow students to work cooperatively.

◆ Because one right answer determined by one correct method is typically the norm, risk taking is discouraged.

◆ Even teachers who maintain orderly, disciplined classrooms often worry that students will be distracted by manipulatives—that they will play instead of work. In addition, both cooperative work and the use of mathematical tools like dice and pattern blocks involve noise, which simply goes against the grain of teachers accustomed to having students work quietly.

Simply put, teachers can do a lot to improve their classrooms for mathematics learning by applying what they already know about successful literacy-learning classrooms. Let's look at how you can make this transfer in four broad areas of pedagogy: designing the classroom environment, scheduling and pacing mathematics lessons, using curriculum for effective planning, and managing the classroom for rigor and risk taking.

Designing the Classroom Environment

The way we set up our classrooms is incredibly important. When we decide how we are going to lay out furniture and store materials, we are making powerful decisions about how students will work, who will be in charge of the paper, and what is most important in our classrooms. When a teacher's desk gives way for ample meeting rugs (and a teacher's tools are relocated to a shelf or a closet), we are saying a lot about where we plan to do most of our work. We won't be spending our days behind our own desks. We will be joining our students in the meeting area or visiting them where they work.

Classrooms set up for reading and writing workshops have a predictable layout: tables or desks are set up in small groups; there is ample space for class meetings, often with a rug; and students can help themselves to a generous supply of appropriate reading and writing materials. This setup is also ideal for mathematics learning. Tables or clusters of desks invite collaboration; a meeting area supports the use of minilessons and facilitates students' math talk. By making math materials (manipulatives, calculators, number charts, and measurement tools) easily accessible, teachers communicate the importance of mathematics learning and provide the means for students to begin learning the critical skill of self-regulation.

Fostering the Independent Use of Manipulatives

Teachers know that for reading, it is not sufficient to merely display lots of books in the classroom: students need explicit instruction and practice on how to handle and select appropriate books. Likewise, students need explicit instruction on how to handle manipulatives and other math tools: how to take them out, how to use them appropriately, and how to put them away. Rubber bands for geoboards may not go airborne; math tools cannot be thrown or tossed around. Calculators should be cleared, closed, and covered as necessary. Cards should be mixed, turned to face the same way, and carefully bundled. The list goes on.

Students also need repeated opportunities to explore learning materials—that is, to play. Few people can make directed use of a new tool without getting a feel for it first, and there is no better way for children to become familiar with a new object than freely playing with it. No matter what the grade—kindergarten through fifth—I spend the first week of school giving students some time to refamiliarize themselves with the math tools I expect them to use that year. I know that pattern blocks, calculators, and base ten materials are inherently mathematical; in the course of their play my students will inadvertently explore such concepts as symmetry, fractions, part-to-whole relationships, place value, and pattern (in addition to the inevitable testing of gravity!). After free exploration of math materials, my youngest students talk about what they discovered, while my older students write about their discoveries.

Once freely explored, various manipulatives become as available to students as the different papers offered for writing. On some days we may all be exploring fractions using geoboards, but on other days students have free access to whatever math materials they need to tackle a multistep problem, whether they be calculators, counters, or number charts.

Time spent playing with manipulatives is well spent; manipulatives are serious and effective learning tools. Just as readers make much better sense of a reading strategy when it is modeled with a real text, children make much better sense of abstract math concepts when they can attach them to concrete examples. Though we can talk about five (count to five or refer to five apples, five cents, and five minutes) and write the number combinations that make five (such as 2 + 3 and 4 + 1), students gain a deeper understanding of five and its parts when they build it with manipulatives like color tiles or stacking cubes. Children who are asked to find the different ways to make five using two colors of stacking cubes, for example, have the opportunity to represent this abstract value with real objects. When students follow this by transferring their work to paper and adding the number combinations represented, students not only practice addition, but build a visual and tactile sense of the number five. That's powerful!

Older students also benefit from exploring and representing mathematical concepts with concrete objects. When my fourth graders explored all possible candy box arrays, they made excellent use of color tiles to discover factor pairs, prime numbers, and square numbers.

Creating a Math-Rich Learning Environment

Highly effective classrooms for reading are also print rich. In addition to the traditional alphabet line, these rooms have prominent word walls, student writing, class-made charts, and well-labeled supplies.

Similarly, math-rich environments optimize mathematics learning. The number line, for example, is a vital tool, useful in helping students visualize number sequences, practice counting, and even solve addition and subtraction problems. Teachers may have several number lines in their rooms: a large commercial one posted before the first day of school, a class-made, growing one that models the number of days in a session, and individual ones at students' work places.

Because students in the upper-elementary grades are expanding their knowledge of the number system in several directions, number lines continue to play an important and significant role. Upper-elementary students are beginning to think about and use numbers into the thousands and millions. They are exploring the numbers between whole numbers (fractions, decimals, and percents) and learning about numbers less than zero. Number lines that include fractions (and show their relations to whole numbers) or go below zero help children develop a mental model that they can refer to to visualize the magnitude of a number, imagine where it fits in a sequence of numbers, and develop mental computation strategies. Number charts also help students illustrate their developing understanding of how numbers in the thousands, ten thousands, and hundred thousands build on the basic base ten system.

A 1–100 chart with pockets for numbers is another visual model of our number system and a valuable tool for exploring place value, patterns in our number system, and strategies for adding and subtracting. As a teacher who has spent time in each of the elementary grades, I have had firsthand experience with the power of the 1–100 chart. I was fascinated to see how even five-year-olds could use this chart to figure out the identities of mystery numbers—counting forward, backward, and even up and down columns to figure out what was under the mystery card. Second graders used the chart to add and subtract, and third graders explored patterns in multiples. Students in the upper grades used 1–100 charts to model computation strategies and extend their thinking about numbers in the hundreds and thousands.

In addition to number lines and charts, math-rich classrooms may include such mathematical tools as calendars, thermometers, and clocks. Prominent display and frequent use of these everyday tools help students see the inherent usefulness of numbers. After all, these tools help us answer very important questions: How many days until Julia's birthday? How long can we play until we must clean up for lunch? Is it too cold to play outside at recess? Older students can begin using calendars and clocks to plan the use of their time and track daily morning temperature readings (great support for learning about seasonal changes).

Besides tools, mathematical language belongs on classroom walls. To foster independent reading and writing, teachers often maintain growing word walls. When students know or learn a word, it goes up on the wall. To support mathematical learning, teachers may include color-coded mathematical terms on their word walls, make a math word chart, or even create a separate word wall just for math.

Math-rich classrooms also have mathematical *thinking* prominently displayed. Such thinking may be embedded in the form of class charts or graphs, student work, or descriptions of student thinking. Prominently post students' work, but take care not to post graded or scored work. Instead of emphasizing how many questions students answered correctly, emphasize work that helps students adopt effective and accurate sense-making strategies. Aim to display work that reflects the thinking, questioning, and problem solving of all students in the classroom.

In my fifth-grade classroom, space above the chalkboard was reserved for my students' written instructions for various computation strategies. For example, after the class helped Darius and his partner, Meghan, edit their instructions for using a halving and doubling strategy for multiplication, they recopied their work and I posted it on the wall. Displayed as such, it became a handy reference for the whole class.

Of course, you need to continually update the math-related materials displayed your classroom. You know how easily print in the classroom can become stale, irrelevant, or developmentally inappropriate for students; the same is true for math-related print in a classroom. It is critical that the mathematical print around the room remain relevant and applicable to classroom use. Examples of literacy- and mathematics-related print in the classroom include the following:

Literacy-Related Print in the Classroom	Mathematics-Related Print in the Classroom
alphabet line	number line (commercial or homemade, growing number line)
word wall	
word families	1–100 chart
class-made charts from content area studies	calendar
class-made charts from whole-group lessons	lists of math vocabulary or a word wall for math (or the inclusion of math words on the regular word wall)
literacy lessons (word families)	
labels on supplies	class-made graphs
labels on book baskets	class-made charts from whole-group math lessons
poems the class has read	students' explanations of computation strategies
quotes from students	
lists of recommended books	student theories and key questions about mathematics
	thermometer
	student height chart
	numbered cubbies
	labels on baskets with math tools

Creating a Classroom That Helps All Students Succeed

I try to make sure my classroom has elements that help all my students, including those who struggle and those who excel. In Chapter 7, I discuss elements of the classroom that are especially helpful for struggling students. However, the classroom environment needs to support my strongest math students as well. Children who easily master grade-level material are at risk for boredom at best and alienation at worst. I need to be sure I consider their needs when I set up my classroom and plan my lessons. I ask myself questions such as: "What extension activities are available?" "For a lesson concerning material that my advanced students have clearly mastered, what other activity choices can I offer?" and "Can I make the day's assignment more challenging by adding a constraint (*You must use at least three operations.*) or requiring more solutions (*Find at least ten ways to show fifty percent on the geoboard.*)?"

Scheduling and Pacing Lessons

Effective literacy instruction requires consistently large chunks of everyday time. In order to become successful readers and writers, students need daily opportunities to practice what they are learning. These opportunities include the use of spontaneous teachable moments that arise each day; teachers use such moments to teach students exactly the literacy skills and understanding they need. In addition, daily classroom routines are skillfully woven into literacy activities.

Likewise, effective mathematics instruction requires large chunks of everyday time. Though classroom instructional time is limited, we can draw conclusions about how to schedule mathematics instruction by looking at effective literacy instruction:

◆ *Allocate time.* Students need daily instruction in mathematics concepts and skills. A solid chunk of time—at least forty-five minutes for kindergartners and up to an hour and a half for upper-elementary students—allows time for teachers to present a lesson, for students to practice or explore the mathematics at hand, and for the class to reflect on its developing understanding. This time is most productive early on in the day; too often math is the last topic of the day—a difficult time for anyone in the classroom (teachers included) to focus on challenging cognitive tasks. Give math at least a couple of morning slots.

◆ *Go outside the math lesson.* Students need opportunities to practice their math skills outside of the daily lesson. This may happen as a separate session of math games or at intervals between lessons (students waiting in a cafeteria line can practice skip-counting, for example). My upper-grade students get a lot of mileage out of skip-counting around the room—a five-minute math activity. They also log a lot of computation practice by doing three problems each morning before our first formal lesson of the day. During literacy, social studies, and science lessons, students use math organically and productively to figure out how many pages they are reading daily, visualize how much space each of the 102 Mayflower passengers had on the 80-foot boat (24 feet across at its widest part), or sort and categorize different species of butterflies.

◆ *Meet students where they are.* Effective mathematics teaching meets students where they are. Teachers need to be attuned to students' individual needs and prepared to address them in spontaneous math lessons, both within the math period and outside it. I taught a lot of math when I helped a kindergartner decide if she had enough money to buy a cupcake at the bake sale and helped a fifth grader figure out how many more books he needed to read in order to fulfill our school's requirement.

◆ *Integrate math into life.* Mathematics should be part of the daily life of the classroom. After all, math is integral to our daily lives: we use math to manage time, plan for the weather, spend (and save!) money, cook, create art, get from here to there, and so on. Students benefit from seeing the daily usefulness of the math they are learning. In effective classrooms, teachers emphasize math's place in our lives. In doing so, we can sneak a lot of other rich math (graphing, problem solving, and estimating) into these routines, as the following table exemplifies:

Integrating Math with Daily Classroom Routines

TIME	*Grades K–1:* Give five-minute warnings before transitions (and really make them five minutes!). Help students see what a minute feels like by jumping, drawing stars, closing their eyes, and so on for one minute. Mention and point out specific times on the clock: "We have fifteen minutes until lunch." "It is one o'clock—time for read-aloud!"

Grades 2–3: Use the clock purposefully to manage time. Post small clock faces in connection with the daily schedule.

Grades 4–5: Ask students to manage their own time during work periods; have them set goals for reading and other projects.

WEATHER

Grades K–1: Students take note of the weather each day and record features (sunny, cloudy, raining, etc.) on a bar, tally, or pictograph. Discuss the graph periodically.

Grades 2–3: Students record daily temperatures and keep track on a line graph. Discuss the graph periodically.

Grades 4–5: Students track temperature, sunrise and sunset, and/or tides, and look at trends through the seasons. Local information can be compared with information from a distant place.

CALENDAR

Grades K–1: Present whole calendars and use them to keep track of important events (trips, birthdays, holidays, special school events). Students talk about "How many days since …?" and "How many days until …?" Make an effort to refer to *today*, *yesterday*, and *tomorrow* on the calendar in the context of daily classroom life.

Grades 2–3: Use calendars to track the number of days of school and prepare for upcoming events (class celebrations, trips, holidays, etc.).

Grades 4–5: Students use the calendar to do long-term planning.

ATTENDANCE/LUNCH

Grades K–1: Students participate in whole-class discussions regarding the number of present and absent students. Each child indicates that he's present by signing in or moving an attendance card. Individual students may report to the class the number of absent and present students and confirm with a head count. Students may also assist in taking a school lunch count and reporting it to the appropriate school personnel.

Grades 2–3: Students may indicate that they're present by participating in a class graph. While discussing the data, students note the number of children participating and the number absent.

Grades 4–5: Students collect attendance data daily and record it on a bar graph. Students periodically discuss trends in attendance: "Why was it so bad that week in February?" "What happens right before and right after a vacation?"

SNACKS/TREATS

Grades K–1: Students count out and serve snacks. They may nibble crackers into different geometric shapes.

Grades 2–3: When served small snacks (fish crackers or raisins), students can estimate how many they have in their hand.

Grades 4–5: Students use the nutrition information panel to determine how much snack each student gets: *If there are 3 crackers in a serving of Ritz crackers and 50 servings in a box, how many can each student get?*

Using Curriculum for Effective Planning: The Three "Knows"

In effective literacy classrooms, teachers draw from a wide variety of excellent materials. To do so, they use students' needs and interests as guides. How does a teacher in today's classroom apply such practices to mathematics?

First, teachers must tackle the three "knows":

1. *Know the math you teach.* Teachers need to know the math they teach and it is often much more complex than it appears. Place value, for one, is an extremely complex, abstract (and interesting) concept. As adults, understanding our number system is such second nature, it is almost impossible to remember that it is not just the way things are. In fact, our number system—albeit extremely clever and useful—is not natural. It is a human-created, systematic way to represent all quantities symbolically (much more practical and easier to calculate with than Roman numerals, for example). In coming to understand the way we organize and represent numbers, children need to learn the meaning and importance of a digit's position (place value) *and* understand that it is based on repeated groupings of ten. This is quite a task! In *Math Matters*, Suzanne Chapin and Art Johnson explain it this way:

   > *These two characteristics, place value and groupings by ten, require students to interpret numerals within numbers on two levels: place value and face value. The 5 in 58 has a place value representing the tens place; the face value of the 5 must therefore be interpreted to mean that five groups of ten, not five ones, are being considered. (2006, 25)*

   To get a better sense of just how challenging it is to learn our base ten system, try exploring a base five system. Pretend, for example, that there is a planet where creatures have developed a counting system based on groupings of five. They would represent our seven as twelve!

   You shouldn't feel daunted by the prospect of gaining a deeper understanding of the math you teach. Though it is of course useful to engage in some study, whether it is through professional development activities or your own personal reading, you can gain an enormous amount of information by simply learning alongside your students. By thinking of themselves as teachers and learners, educators have relearned fractions, division, algebra, and probability—topics that are often preceded by a past of little or no understanding. Elementary teachers often find that they are exploring alternative strategies for basic addition and multiplication *with* their students, and it is not unusual for these teachers to gain a new interest and appreciation for math in the process. Though in many cases our fondness of literacy may trump our fondness of math, it is critical that we stay open to a deeper understanding of the math we teach. This knowledge is essential in setting goals—that is, determining just what we need to teach. Along the way, you'll often find that you like math much more than you once thought!

2. *Know your math curriculum.* Teachers need to know their mandated math curriculum. It is difficult to supplement, complement, or otherwise change curriculum until you are clear on just how it works. This is especially true when the structure or approaches are unfamiliar or new.

3. *Know your students.* Teachers need to know their students. In order to get the students from *here* (where they are) to *there* (the mathematical goals set for them), teachers need to know each student's starting point. Teachers have long been aware that students come to math with different experiences and degrees of understanding and ability. Ongoing assessments of students help teachers fluidly group students according to their changing needs.

As you become familiar with your curriculum and your students' needs, you also need a repertoire of good resources from which to draw appropriate games, lessons, activities, and projects.

I am indebted to the core curriculum I use. It provides a sound and solid scope and sequence for the math I teach, and the lessons are terrific. Still, in one way or another my students always let me know it's not sufficient. Those students who get math easily crave a challenge. On the other hand, students who struggle to make sense of our daily math lessons need supportive activities to build up their understanding (and their confidence). And the class as a whole benefits when, inspired by a juicy mathematical curiosity, we take a detour from our regular curriculum to investigate.

Managing Mistakes and Encouraging Risk Taking

Teachers working with young readers and writers make great use of student errors. In fact, in reading lessons, what used to be *mistakes* are now called *miscues*—that is, cues to student thinking. We seek insights into students' thinking so that we can learn what they know and how their understanding is developing. By examining students' reading and writing errors, we learn if a student is attending to meaning, hearing all parts of a word, being aware of rhymes, developing a sight-word vocabulary, and more. Errors show what students can do as well as what they cannot; they are a crucial part of a child's learning process.

We encourage students to attempt their own spelling when they write. We may ask young children to do this to facilitate beginning writing. Older students may estimate the spelling of an unusual word when they are drafting or note taking to maintain the flow of their work. While no teacher would discourage a student capable of using conventional spelling fluently, and all students will need to make the transition from approximate spellings to standardized ones, this practice of estimating or inventing their own spelling serves several important purposes:

◆ students build the ability to write independently;

◆ students make use of a vocabulary well beyond their conventional spelling ability;

◆ students develop phonemic awareness (a key early literacy concept); and

◆ students learn that making errors is an inevitable, appropriate part of the learning process.

We want to encourage the same willingness to experiment when our students are doing math. For example, miscue analysis of students' calculation strategies helps us see their understanding (and misunderstanding) of arithmetic and of place value. When I ask students to explain wrong answers, I often find out that their thinking was in fact sound, and that they had just hit a glitch. And when I ask students to explain *right* answers, I sometimes learn that their thinking was not so robust—they may have gotten a right answer by luck or with shaky understanding.

For example, a student may be competent in executing a well-practiced algorithm but have no other way to explain why her answer is correct. A second grader, Aliana, approached me with her math paper to ask the dreaded question: "Is this right?" She had set up an addition problem, 48 + 54, and solved it with the traditional carrying algorithm. Her answer was correct.

"What do you think?" I asked.

"Well, I did it the right way, so it must be right," she reasoned.

Hmm. I probed a bit. "Could it be ninety-two?"

"Maybe," she said, exploring my face for a clue.

"Let's see if we can find a way to help you be more sure," I suggested. It was important for Aliana to be more confident about what those numbers represented and how the traditional algorithm really worked, especially if she was going to continue using it. It would be no help to her understanding if I simply gave her the answer; the correctness of her answer had to be apparent to her.

When I stopped by to see how Calvin was doing on the same problem, I noticed that his paper was a mess and his answer was wrong. "How did you solve that, Calvin?" I inquired.

"Well, I knew it was going to be close to hundred, because both numbers are pretty close to fifty. Then I saw that forty-eight was two away from fifty, so I took two from fifty-four. It's easier to add onto fifty," Calvin explained.

"I agree," I answered. "So tell me what you did to get your answer."

Calvin launched into an explanation, full of confidence. Suddenly he stopped.

"Wait a minute . . . ," he pondered. "I made a mistake." Calvin turned to his work and corrected the error he had made. I learned a lot in guiding Calvin through his thinking. He was full of confidence, had a good sense of the magnitude of numbers, and came up with great strategies for addition, but he needed a bit of work on organizing his thoughts on paper.

Because students' errors, attempts, and approximations are often our best guides for planning, it is critical that children allow us to see and make use of the mistakes they will inevitably make. Making mistakes in front of others is not easy! We have to work hard to help our students feel safe enough to make mistakes publicly. To do so, we should always keep the following four practices in mind:

◆ *Value thinking processes as well as correct answers.* For example, when I ask, "How did you solve the problem?" in the process of announcing their answer, my students focus on how they came to it. The importance of the accuracy of the answer *and* the effectiveness of the strategy is emphasized.

◆ *Value problems for which more than one answer is possible.* For example, when a teacher asks, "What numbers can we add together to get a sum of fourteen?" different correct responses are possible. Again, the importance of both the accuracy of the answer and the strategy is emphasized.

◆ *Value inquisitive responses.* When students present an answer, instead of responding, "Right," or "Wrong," press students to find proof in the math they used. Ask questions like "Can you explain your thinking?"

◆ *Value tolerance for mistakes.* You shouldn't tolerate when students tease, roll their eyes, or utter exasperating comments like "That's easy!" when they learn of an individual student's mistake. You may need to enforce this rigorously, but over time you'll find that students stop seeing mistake making as embarrassing. Respect for thinking develops into respect for thinkers.

It is important to emphasize that encouraging risk taking does not mean accuracy is irrelevant or secondary. The ability to be accurate in mathematics is essential. As important as accuracy is, however, if students don't have a robust understanding of the way they are attaining right answers, they are simply not working on solid ground. If we hope to provide students with a strong foundation for higher mathematics, understanding will have to be as essential as accuracy. When students determine the accuracy of their answers by examining their thinking processes, they improve the likelihood of being right in the future.

The Whole Picture

Common sense applies: good teaching practices in one subject area are likely to be equally good in another. By setting up our classrooms to foster independence, creativity, differentiation, and risk taking, we set the tone for exemplary work in any subject.

FROM READING TO MATH TO YOUR CLASSROOM

1. *What do you think are the essential elements of a successful reading classroom? Are they essential in the math classroom as well? If so, how can you make sure they are present?*

2. *What might you do to increase your knowledge of the math you teach, the curriculum you use, and your students?*

3. *What are some other ways that you can integrate math learning into the rest of your day?*

The Workshop Model

If you have well-established reading and writing workshops, chances are your students think of themselves as readers and writers. However, this identification may not carry over to math time, with your students seeing themselves as either good at math or not. Have you ever thought about trying to implement a math workshop in your classroom but weren't quite sure how to accomplish it?

M r. Brown, my fifth-grade teacher, really knew how to teach. He had a warm sense of humor, a genuine affection for kids, and a gift for curriculum. He would cluster us in groups to work on social studies and science projects (highlights included a board game of the human circulatory system and a scale model of a Colonial village). Reading instruction was centered on well-chosen read-alouds, and we sat in book clubs to discuss our personal reading. We learned math facts with engaging games that Mr. Brown invented, and he took obvious delight in witnessing his students' creative mathematical processes. At a time when most students sat in rows completing responses to writing prompts, Mr. Brown met one-on-one with each of us to talk about our personal writing. He also took the time to have us share our finished work with our classmates. Mr. Brown was a deeply human teacher who helped me through a hard time in my life with gentle grace and patient kindness.

I will never forget him; I am a teacher now in part because of his influence.

Great teaching has been around for a long time, and for a long time teachers have been passing on their success stories. Unfortunately, in the effort to explain what works and what doesn't, we've managed to get tangled in a lot of jargon that labels our teaching practices. Mr. Brown did not invent cooperative work, math games, book clubs, conferring, publishing, or sharing, and I seriously doubt he thought in these educational terms. Nonetheless, the practices were evident—and successful—in his teaching. I do know that Mr. Brown worked closely with Mrs. Burnett (they team-taught a mixed-aged fifth- and sixth-grade class in 1974) and that he was a true student of his craft. He learned from other teachers, innovated his own practices, and passed on what worked. He is an outstanding model of what great teachers have always done, regardless of what it's labeled.

These days teachers often feel bombarded by a constant stream of new approaches, mandates, and curricula. Despite the fact that most new approaches are thoughtful outgrowths of old ones, labeling them anew makes it, at times, feel like the wheel is being reinvented. We become fatigued—and perhaps dismissive of them—as a result. However, while it is understandable that we may be a bit wary of the next big thing, the next big thing is always worth investigating.

One contemporary term in literacy education is *the workshop model*. According to *Merriam-Webster's Online Dictionary* (n.d.), a workshop is "a usually brief intensive educational program for a relatively small group of people that focuses especially on techniques and skills in a particular field" or "a small establishment where manufacturing or handicrafts are carried on." In the elementary classroom, the workshop is a place where students are busily engaged in intensive study of skills and manufacturing of understanding. There is an understanding that students will have their *hands on* their learning, and that they are, in many respects, acting as apprentices to adult readers, writers, and mathematicians. They are doing reading, writing, and math.

While the term *workshop model* means different things to different teachers, what is consistent is that the workshop includes instruction, practice, and reflection. One teacher may include a daily minilesson, time for independent practice with conferring, and a whole-group share or reflection. Another teacher's workshop may start with a mini-lesson two or three times a week and include a combination of independent reading and book clubs or partnerships with daily guided reading groups. Teachers have found this model effective in a number of subjects, from physical education to French, and it is certainly well suited to the teaching and learning of mathematics. This chapter focuses on how the literacy workshop model for structuring lessons supports independence, understanding, and differentiation in math. Let's first look at how the workshop model works in literacy.

The Literacy Workshop

The workshop approach to teaching reading and writing has been developed—and continues to be refined—to address the complex goals of literacy learning:

◆ to become competent in decoding and encoding;

◆ to acquire a repertoire of strategies for comprehending a wide range of literary genres;

◆ to develop the ability to talk and write about reading and writing; and

◆ to make reading and writing lifelong interests.

The last goal, though it sounds touchy-feely, is critical. Because reading and writing are essential to disseminating information and developing the capacity for critical thinking, unless we succeed in getting our students engaged in reading and writing, our efforts are futile. To that end, teachers regard making their students into *readers* and *writers* as one of the most important goals of their profession.

Though various teachers' reading and writing workshops may look a bit different, they include similar components. First and foremost, effective reading and writing workshops include time for reading and writing. Students must have plenty of time to read and write in ways that are engaging and personally relevant. The centerpiece of the literacy workshop—independent reading and writing—meets this need. Because students require direct instruction to become readers and writers, teachers have embedded several structures for instruction within this model.

A literacy workshop generally lasts sixty to ninety minutes and may contain a number of the following components (though all contain independent reading and writing):

Components of a Literacy Workshop

MINILESSONS
These brief lessons, lasting roughly fifteen to twenty-five minutes, provide direct instruction in reading or writing strategies that children are likely to find useful at the time.

INDEPENDENT READING OR WRITING
During this chunk of time, ranging from fifteen minutes for kindergartners to forty-five minutes or more for upper-grade students, students read books or write on topics largely of their own choice. There is a strong emphasis on doing work that makes sense: reading books that are at a student's independent reading level and using invented spelling along with conventional spelling.

CONFERRING
Teachers sit alongside readers and writers as they work. Teachers research and understand what the students are working on, then teach based on what they have gathered from these more personal moments.

GUIDED READING GROUPS OR STRATEGY LESSONS
Teachers work with small, fluid groups organized around a similar reading level or shared need (to review a particular comprehension strategy, for example, or how to incorporate dialogue in a piece of writing).

WORD STUDY
Students work on spelling patterns, word recognition, vocabulary, and phonics.

CENTERS AND BOOK CLUBS
Centers, usually used with younger students, and book clubs, for older readers, provide partner or small-group experiences in reading. These structured activities engage students in reading and talking about books together.

WRITING OR READING SHARE
Workshops conclude by highlighting the learning students did during independent reading and writing. The share is more than just an opportunity for students to be proud of what they have done; teachers emphasize this time as a teaching and learning opportunity. By repeating the teaching point, teachers give students another shot at making sense of the day's lesson.

Though these structures are not exactly new, educators have worked hard to refine them in the context of the workshop model, making certain that there is time for independent practice. Teachers who structure their classrooms around the workshop model also emphasize student choice, inquiry, and fluid grouping of students.

In the classroom, the workshop model helps me meet the diverse and crucial goals of developing students' enthusiasm, skills, and knowledge base. A workshop is different from a lesson because the children are more than students; they are beholders of grand jobs—readers, writers, mathematicians, historians, and more. Over time, and with plenty of support, I hand responsibility over to my students. With my guidance, my younger readers and writers choose their books and select the right kind of paper for the writing they are planning. Older kids set goals for their reading and select the best revision strategy for their written piece from the ones we've studied. They study their reading rates and discuss strategies for improving them. Moreover, they learn to take an interest in each other's reading and writing, and they help each other develop their literacy skills and enthusiasm for reading and writing.

The Mathematics Workshop

Goals in mathematics are similar to the goals of literacy workshops. I want my students to not only be literate in mathematical comprehension—that is, be able to read mathematical situations and understand them—but be *skilled* in mathematics as well. Moreover, it is crucial that students develop an affinity for mathematical thinking. In an increasingly technological, data-driven world, it is critical that we support students in becoming mathematically empowered workers and citizens. Those of us who love mathematics cherish the goal of introducing students to the beautiful logic of number, space, and data, with the hopes that they will embrace and enjoy this form of thinking, too.

Because in many ways goals in mathematics closely mirror those in literacy, teachers have successfully adopted the workshop model to structure their mathematics lessons. In creating a workshop approach to teaching mathematics, teachers have developed structures very similar to those in the literacy workshop. Components of the mathematics workshop include the following:

Components of a Mathematics Workshop (at a Glance)

minilessons or other whole-group lessons

independent work on mathematics

time to explore and practice how numbers work

guided small-group support or strategy lessons

conferring

group work: structures for collaboration, talk, and choice

math shares (reflection)

Let's address each of these components in detail, in the order they are listed above.

Minilessons or Other Whole-Group Lessons

Most math workshops begin with a whole-group lesson during which the teacher introduces or reviews concepts, models skills, and gives instructions. In teaching literacy, teachers have used the term *minilesson* to describe both the brevity of the lesson and the narrow specificity of the lesson's topic. A well-constructed and well-delivered literacy mini-lesson can last from only five to a more genous twenty minutes, leaving a solid chunk of time for independent work.

Because school time is limited, and the need for independent work is great, brief lessons are an effective tool. Most mathematics topics are way too big to learn in a lesson or two, and students are much better off exploring them over many days. Doing so via brief lessons is stimulating as well as effective. Teachers reserve the right to have longer whole-group lessons, including more extensive classroom discussions, when the topic warrants it. In math, minilessons tend to be longer, but still focused enough to leave time and opportunity for students to work in partnerships, small groups, or on their own (independent of their teachers). After this work, they share their thinking with others.

A well-constructed math minilesson is wonderful to observe: fifteen to twenty-five minutes of skillful teaching energizes students and sets them on their way to independent work. Like any piece of great teaching, minilessons take practice. It is useful to study the four-step structure of successful minilessons:

Step 1: The Connection: how the day's lesson relates to the ongoing work

Step 2: The Teaching: direct instruction of a new strategy or skill

Step 3: Active Engagement: students make an initial attempt to use the new teaching

Step 4: The Link: students see how they will apply the lesson's teaching to the day's work

Let's look at each of these steps in depth.

Minilesson Step 1: The Connection
A successful minilesson begins by connecting the day's work to the larger context of the unit—what students did they day before or the work they are about to do. Remember, time is of essence. As Lucy Calkins notes in *The Art of Teaching Reading* (2001), we should avoid the kind of low-level questions we are accustomed to asking ("Who can remember what we did yesterday?" "What do we call the top number in a fraction? It starts *Nnn* . . ." "Who knows what *percent* means?"). These "read my mind" questions tend to take a lot of time, and though they may let us know who is paying attention, who has a good memory, and who can guess what the teacher wants the student to say, their purpose fails to go much deeper. In launching a minilesson, you'll be better off laying out the connection to the previous day's math work: "Yesterday I noticed that at lot of you were used to thinking of fractions as pieces of a shape, like a pie or a pizza. Today we are going to explore a different way to think about fractional parts: we are going to compare them with percentages." Or "I was so excited by the way Jasmine was thinking about equivalent fractions that I had to share it with you. It will really help you with today's work."

Minilesson Step 2: The Teaching
In the next phase of a minilesson, teachers teach the content of the lesson. In literacy, this usually means teaching a strategy or skill that

will be useful to the students' reading and writing—and hopefully applied that same day. In mathematics, it is the teaching necessary for the students to engage in the day's independent math work. The lesson may include defining new vocabulary or introducing new concepts; it will almost always include modeling on the teacher's part. In teaching a minilesson on comparing fractions with their percent equivalents to fifth graders, I jot numbers on a board or chart paper while saying: "Any fractional part can also be named as a percentage. One-half can be called fifty percent. This is a really nice landmark; it can help me figure out others. For example, I know that one-fourth will be twenty-five percent because a fourth is a half of one-half and twenty-five is half of fifty."

The teaching phase may include asking some students to try out the same strategy while the rest observe. For example, I ask my class, "What about three-fourths? Anyone want to try using what we have figured out so far to find the percent equivalent for three-fourths?" Again, I find it helpful to avoid quizlike questions ("Who remembers what *percent* means?") in favor of simply supplying any necessary or useful information ("It might help you to remember that *percent* actually means 'out of one hundred.'"). I might choose a more open-ended question to engage students: "Who can explain how I figured out the percent equivalent of one-fourth?"

Minilesson Step 3: Active Engagement
The teaching step is followed by active student engagement. Because it is impossible to assess which students have gotten it by simply listening to my lesson (and highly likely that many have not), I have found it critical to introduce some form of student engagement. Students are more likely to be successful independently if they actively try the strategy in the meeting area before heading off to work on their own. This step also gives me the opportunity to address and clear up confusion.

Active engagement may take several forms, as long as the focus remains on the involvement of every student. You might ask students to mentally work on a sample problem, respond to it in their math journals, or work on a dry-erase board ("Try one on your own now. What would be the percent equivalent of one-eighth?"). Partners may work on a sample problem with each other ("Turn and talk to your partner: What is the percent equivalent of one-eighth?").

After students have had the opportunity to be engaged on their own or in partners, we make their work public. There are a number of options here. First, simply asking students to share their thinking is an extremely rich and effective teaching move. We hear their thinking about fraction and percent relationships and can assess their ability to explain their reasoning. Student explanations serve as clarifications for each other as well: children often understand each other *better* than they understand us.

Sometimes we ask students to share a partner's thinking. This move supports students whose original ideas were shaky but who got a lot out of listening to a math partner. It also supports development of strong listening skills—an essential learning and life skill.

Sometimes we want to expedite this public moment and save discussion for after students have had more time to explore mathematical skills and concepts. At these times, the teacher might do the sharing ("While you were talking with your partners, I heard Suzanne and Alphonse say that since one-eighth was half of one-fourth, its percent equivalent would be half of twenty-five"). Or the teacher may talk about what he hoped kids would be doing ("How many of you used the percent equivalent of one-fourth to help you?"). However students' thinking is elicited, it provides an important opportunity to see if kids are ready to work on their own. If there is considerable confusion, the teacher can return to teaching and then revisit active engagement. If she hasn't already, the teacher might bring in manipulatives or other visual representations. Or she might chose a more simplified version ("Let's talk about how knowing the percent equivalent of one-tenth can help you figure out the percent equivalent of three-tenths."). If confusion is limited to a smaller group of students, the teacher may elect to work with them when the rest of the kids are independently engaged.

Minilesson Step 4: The Link
The final stage of literacy minilessons prepares students to start the day's independent reading or writing. In mathematics, most often students will be expected to apply the skill just modeled or explore the concept just introduced. This last step is a clarification of logistics: you might tell students where and with whom they will work, what supplies they may need, and exactly what they should accomplish

during the independent work period. I often end my minilessons by listing on the board the steps students should take to get started on their work for the day.

As previously mentioned, math minilessons last roughly fifteen to twenty-five minutes. Teachers can pack a powerful punch in this tight time frame, and the time they have saved can be better spent after the day's independent work. Students are often better prepared to engage in a class discussion after they have had a chance to explore the math independently.

I find that there is no substitute for practicing minilessons, especially to improve upon keeping them clear and brief. I also know that I am easily diverted by a student's interesting comment and sometimes detour the class into a long, albeit interesting conversation. Though I reserve the right to do this when it seems worthwhile, I have also enlisted my students' help by telling them, "This meeting should last only about twenty minutes, and we should be off the rug by ten thirty-five." My older students help me keep an eye on the time, while younger ones tell me when "the big hand is on the seven."

Independent Work on Mathematics

You can definitely *not* hear a pin drop when my kindergartners and first graders are hard at work doing math. The classroom is a busy, active place. On any given day students might be working with partners to find out what $9 + 9$ is (and providing solid proof for their answer on paper), working independently to tally the combinations they made when they rolled two dice, or working their way through a menu of activities that explores early concepts in geometry. One might hear developmentally appropriate bickering ("He took my pencil!") and even off-task talk ("Who is your favorite Power Ranger?"), but most of the noise is math focused—the sounds of dice falling, excited voices sharing results, and partners cheering and laughing ("Seven won again!").

Just as actually doing reading and writing is essential to learning them, so is doing math—and doing plenty of it. The independent focus of a math workshop shares the same criteria as independent literacy work: there is plenty of time on task, there are elements of student choice, and the math is at a just-right (independent) level for each student. This independent work period may include partner or small-group activities, problems, games, and assignments for students to do individually.

Choice

Because interest plays such a critical part in developing reading and writing skills, choice is an important component of literacy workshops. Though there are inevitable limitations (students may not be allowed to write pieces that demean other students; they may be required to write poetry; or they may have to read at a particular level), teachers acknowledge that students are often the best judges of what is the right writing topic or book. Because we are always teaching toward the ultimate goal of making regular, intelligent choices about reading and writing, we give students choice early in their development. Of course, this does not preclude teachers from assigning books, stories, or writing topics. We must all be proficient readers and writers of material we don't choose, and many of these genres (such as nonfiction materials and poetry) require specific teaching and learning to be comprehended and appreciated. Regardless, in the workshop model there is always a place for books and writing topics of a student's choice.

Though it remains important, choice looks somewhat different in the math workshop, for example, students are less likely to choose topics for independent study (though some teachers have allowed for this with amazing success). However, students *should* be making choices: activities from a menu, appropriate manipulative materials, problem-solving approaches, games for fact practice, strategies for calculation, and methods of representation. Just as they do in literacy workshops, students in math workshops learn how to make appropriate choices over time and with explicit instruction from their teachers. Above all, teachers and students should strive to make sure the activities, tools, and strategies they choose both make sense mathematically and make sense to the students using them.

Young students benefit when they can choose a variety of materials and strategies to help them solve story problems. When I ask my young students to figure out how many animals went to see the world in Eric Carle's classic picture book *Rooster's Off to See the World* (1972), the children have had experience solving story problems. They have learned that there are lots of math tools that they can use, including—but not limited to—drawings, cubes, fingers, teddy bears, and (for the sophisticated few) tally marks. Some children choose to show the animals that went off to see the world with representational drawings (though the single rooster tends to be a bit more detailed than the five fish). These representations are carefully drawn, labeled, and counted. These students rely on concrete representations to make sense of the problem; the drawings are a successful strategy and often make the most sense to young mathematicians.

Other children might use linking cubes to represent the various animals, then draw the train of cubes to record their work. This approach bridges the concrete with the more abstract. Still others use tally marks on the paper, then label and count them, working yet more abstractly. Finally, the students with the strongest sense of number write number sentences, a very abstract strategy. (**Note:** Though this is indeed very effective and certainly a goal for all students, while students are still developing early number sense, we don't want to push using it.)

As I observe students and visit them at work, I am delighted with the range of strategies they choose. I am also mindful of my job; it is so important that kids move on from drawing when they are ready, and to hold off from using number sentences until they really know what they are doing. I also need to be sure that all kids are doing just-right math and can succeed independently, given the right tools.

Just-Right Levels

Independent activities must have the possibility of being successfully completed independently. Whether students are reading, writing, or doing mathematics, the work should be neither too easy nor too hard, but what literacy teachers refer to as *just right*. For each student there is a range of just-right work: it may be useful to do work that is a little easy (it helps reinforce a developing skill or understanding) or a little too hard (the challenge can be stimulating and rewarding).

Making sure students are doing just-right math takes practice. In reading, teachers assess students, determine their reading levels, and teach them to choose just-right books. Though this requires a lot of knowledge, sophistication, and hard work on the teacher's part, it is a reliable way to ensure students are doing appropriately leveled work.

Writing, too, is relatively easy to differentiate: with conferring and small-group instruction, more able students can be expected to write longer pieces, incorporate more sophisticated revision strategies, and meet higher standards for spelling than those students who are struggling.

In the math workshop, though there will inevitably be a wide range of mathematical abilities, most days there will be one lesson addressing one piece of mathematical content. Effective teachers plan activities that encompass the "a little easy"–to–"a little hard" spectrum. They are also prepared to adapt the work to meet the needs of students who still find it much too hard or much too easy.

When I began teaching, I found meeting the needs of all my students enormously difficult. I tended to support my struggling students by sitting with them as they worked, coaxing them through each problem step-by-step. The results were usually correct answers but rarely much understanding, and often frustration on behalf of my students. It just wasn't working; with that much support they weren't actually doing the math, just doing what I suggested. Though there are times that students have a breakthrough with this kind of hand-holding, more often they simply follow the teacher's prompts and are not really able to do more of the same problems without the same level of support. Over time I learned that to be prepared for those students who are really struggling, I needed to think about adjusting the problem so it is truly independent work. This might mean changing the numbers (for example, using familiar landmark numbers like fifteen or forty, or using two- instead of three-digit numbers), removing a step of a multistep problem, providing a graphic organizer, or supplying additional visual information. Students can also be assigned partners who are doing math at roughly their level and who can puzzle out work that is *a little* hard.

In my first years of teaching I also needed to learn how to plan for students for whom the day's work was likely to be easy. Like other teachers, I often asked them to help others or do additional examples of the same kind of problems. Over time, I found that continually partnering struggling students with quite capable ones was rarely helpful for either, and that doing a lot of problems that are too easy is not any more stimulating than doing just a few. Avid math students may need the day's activity to be more complex. This does not necessarily mean it should involve bigger numbers. Adding more steps, creating messier situations (for example, including remainders to contend with), and providing less information are all ways to challenge more able students' thinking.

You can also encourage avid math students to embark on independent research into mathematical questions that they can work on over time (*How can you tell if a number is divisible by 11 once you get past 99? Or Is there a way to figure out if any given number is prime?*). These kinds of questions defy easy answers and encourage deep mathematical thinking—exploration of patterns, making and testing conjectures, and developing and explaining proofs.

Routines and Extensions

In order to carry out math workshops in which students are truly working independently, you'll have to establish routines. Students need to know how to take out, use, and put away math materials. They need strategies for answering their own questions without having to go to you (asking three students first, for example). They need to know what to do when they get stuck, which may include asking for your help but should include seeking support from other students, too.

Students also need to know what to do when they have finished. Readers who finish one book can start another, and writers who finish their day's assignment can jot an entry in a writer's notebook. When students finish a math task before the independent math period is over, we want them to continue to be engaged in math. Though sometimes doing more of the same activity is useful, it's helpful to develop a repertoire of extension activities:

Extension Activities (After Completion of Independent Work in a Math Workshop)

Students may choose a math game they have learned that addresses a range of abilities (and interests).

Students may engage in free exploration of manipulatives. This is not wasted time; younger students really cannot get enough of pattern blocks and Cuisinaire rods, and older kids benefit from time to mess around with geoboards (a manipulative that may not get frequent use but is rich with mathematics). There is so much math inherent in these materials that students will almost definitely be learning something as they play.

Students may work on mastering facts they have found difficult, using a strategy previously introduced in the workshop.

Time to Explore and Practice How Numbers Work

In literacy workshops, learning includes developing phonics, vocabulary, and spelling awareness. To meet this goal, teachers have created practices to support the learning of such content. These practices are often referred to as *word study* or *word work*. The practices encompass the study of the alphabet, sound-letter correspondence, word families, spelling patterns, and prefixes and suffixes as well as strategies for learning high-frequency words. What makes current word study practices different from traditional spelling instruction is a focus on constructing an *understanding* of phonics and spelling patterns, rather than rote memorization. For example, students in primary grades go on a letter hunt, collecting words that begin with a particular letter, such as C, and then sorting them by sound. By sorting words and making generalizations about them, students learn how words work. This is enormously helpful in building vocabulary, decoding unfamiliar words, and spelling conventionally. And because sorting, categorizing, and pattern seeking are at the heart of word study, this practice is a very mathematical part of the literacy day as well.

Unlike other components of the literacy workshop, word study is not usually done in the workshop period. Though it may be the subject of a strategy group in a writing workshop, it is generally taught at a separate time. On the contrary, in mathematics, the study of number facts and patterns is often the topic of a day's independent work.

In addition to developing deep conceptual understanding of such subjects as place value, probability, and fractions, we must make sure that students understand how numbers work and be able to compute with numbers effectively. Since children must know basic facts and computation strategies in order to engage in any other math, this often takes center stage in the math workshop. This work may include time to explore and study basic facts and computational strategies such as student-created algorithms, traditional algorithms, and other alternative algorithms.

In word study, students explore patterns in word families to help them with both vocabulary development and spelling. In mathematics, students explore fact families. The patterns inherent in addition, subtraction, multiplication, and division lend themselves to rich exploration. Students gain insights that provide a logical rationale for mathematical understanding (such as the associative property of addition and multiplication) and benefit from the repeated exposure to common combinations.

My kindergartners and first graders are fascinated with the exploration of patterns in addition. Our early work with combinations is always linked to real objects. For example, students might explore all the combinations that come up when they toss five two-colored counters. Sometimes they count two yellow and three red; other times they see one yellow and four reds. Occasionally, they have all reds and no yellows. These experiments allow students to record their tosses with simple drawings (coloring five circles), then compile the combinations they find. Next, we work as a class. "What combinations did you toss?" I ask. Eager hands shoot up; maybe a few students, eager to answer, call out. "Wait until I call on you. Maya, you are raising your hand patiently. Can you tell us a combination that you got? Tell me what you got, but make sure you say the reds first."

"I got two reds and three yellows," Maya replies.

I record this on a chart with three different markers: red, yellow, and black for the addition and equal signs. "Did anyone else get the same combination as Maya?" Though I am pretty sure we will hear another child contribute the same combination, this kind of question allows more students to participate and gets all of them focused on their lists. Hands shoot up. "Who got something different?" I ask.

I continue collecting students' responses until it seems that we have exhausted all possibilities. Along the way we examine what I've recorded to make sure we have no repeats. Even with the color-coded number sentences, this is difficult for some kids, because there is so much information in these abstract symbols to make sense of.

Once we have what seems to be a complete list of combinations of five, students go to work at organizing it. Because they love patterns and have lots of experience with counting to ten, they quickly see the way combinations grow from 1 + 4 to 2 + 3 and so on, to 4 + 1. The combinations with zero prove to be trickier, and we work together to find where they fit. Then there are cheers: this is an extremely satisfying lesson, and it leads the way to powerful understanding. We talk about what happened and why there are no other possible combinations. In the future, students will return to the tossing and recording activity, this time including their own number sentences.

Older students may look for patterns in multiples. These may be explored on 1–100 charts, or students may generate lists using calculators, then work together to describe the patterns they find. Students are invariably fascinated to see the way that digits in multiples of 9 add up to 9 and witness how the multiples of 11 appear so easy at first (11, 22, 33, 44 . . .), then suddenly become complicated when 11 is multiplied by a factor higher than 9. When teachers urge students to explain why these patterns emerge, students engage in serious mathematics. In addition, they benefit from the exposure to multiplication facts.

Guided Small-Group Support or Strategy Lessons

During a reading or writing workshop, while students are engaged in independent work, teachers are likely to be doing one of three things: teaching a guided reading group, teaching a small-group strategy lesson, or conferring one-on-one with a reader or writer.

Guided reading is generally used with students in kindergarten through third grade and supports students in becoming independent readers. In guided reading, students practice reading with a teacher's support. Teachers choose books that are on the slightly higher end of the just-right range. They anticipate challenging parts and scaffold the reading efforts of students. This is not round-robin reading; after an introduction to the book by the teacher, students usually read independently and often silently. Students should experience success in guided reading; hence the teacher is there to help. In guided small-group reading, groups are dynamic and change frequently, but they always consist of students at roughly the same level. The goal is to develop skills to read more challenging texts independently. Students work in guided reading groups for about fifteen minutes, and they may do so roughly once a week.

Strategy lessons involve more explicit teaching and are used with students at all elementary grade levels. Small groups are formed around a shared need—to look more closely at word endings, for example, or use prediction as a comprehension strategy. Teachers explain the strategy and support students in practicing it by reading a book that is at their independent reading level. As in guided reading groups, students read independently and the small groups are fluid.

These groups are formed as need arises. A helpful way to form them is to base them on informal assessment done in a minilesson.

These small-group structures are also useful in a math workshop. In doing guided math, you can form small groups of students at a similar level and support them as they do math at the slightly challenging end of the just-right range. You can help students identify tricky spots and highlight their use of effective strategies—that is, serve as a conduit that passes students' own good ideas on to other students ("Did anyone notice how Antonio used the one-to-one-hundred chart to add tens then add the ones?" Or "Let's watch how Giselle is moving the beans as she counts them.")

In applying the strategy group model to math, you may pull a small group together based on the group members' mutual need for a certain strategy. For example, if there is a core group of students who could benefit from rearranging addends to simplify combining them (changing $6 + 5 + 8 + 4 + 2$ into $6 + 4 + 8 + 2 + 5$), give them a customized minilesson on the strategy for combining several addends. You can also use strategy lessons to reinforce or reiterate a minilesson that several students did not get, or on the other hand, nudge along a group of kids who are ready for a challenge.

One year, looking through my fourth graders' work, I took note that a handful of them had not internalized place-value understandings and, as a result, were having difficulty adding larger numbers. The next day, while their classmates were engaged in a problem-solving activity, I pulled this small group together for a strategy lesson. We looked at patterns in tens on the 1–100 chart and on the calculator. We examined and reexamined what happened when we added ten onto a number. These children expressed surprise (and excitement) that the digit in the tens column grew by one while the digit in the ones column stayed the same. After exploring patterns in tens together for a few minutes, I gave the small group problems, such as $43 + 10$, to solve on their own and share with a partner. Because place-value understandings can be so difficult to internalize, and because most fourth graders have usually accomplished it, I was confident it was time well spent. I also knew that this small group would most likely need to return to this topic.

During the fifteen minutes that I focused my attention on this small group, the rest of my students worked on their own. Students were learning that, in such situations, I would be available in time, and they sought other means for finding answers to most of their questions. For my part, I needed to be sure that the vast majority of the kids in the class were set to work on their own. For this reason, unless I had a student teacher in the room, I saved strategy and guided math group work for the second half of the independent work period.

Conferring

When teachers are not working with small groups, they may be talking one-on-one with students, conferring with them about their work in mathematics. Because conferring is such a useful tool for learning about how students work and think, I address it at length in Chapter 6.

Group Work: Structures for Collaboration, Talk, and Choice

Partner and group work differs from regular practice of student talk. Students benefit from sharing their thinking with others, no matter what the curriculum area. Regular student talk can take place before individual work ("Talk with your partner about your goals for the day"), in the midst of individual work ("Stop and talk with your partner—what are you thinking right now?" "What help do you need to keep going today?"), or at the end of a day's individual work ("Before we have our whole-class share, turn to your partner and tell him or her one thing you learned today."). This kind of regular talk helps students stay focused and accountable, and it stretches their thinking. Saying our thoughts out loud helps us notice gaps, errors, and inconsistencies.

In addition to this regular talk, teachers in literacy workshops have crafted partner and small-group assignments to complement the individual work. For example, younger students work with partners to pore over baskets of books sorted by theme (opposites, ABC books, or different versions of the Cinderella tale). Students talk about similarities and differences in a certain kind of books and, in the process, build an understanding of how to read (and write) this type of book. Older students work with partners or book clubs to read and discuss books they have chosen. These may be from a specific genre (such as realistic fiction or fantasy) or related to a specific topic (the American Revolution or environmental issues). Teachers' minilessons are crafted specifically to help the students deepen their comprehension of these genres and topics and improve their ability to discuss them. Students read assigned pages or chapters on their own (during the workshop and at home), plan contributions to book club meetings, and meet with other book club members on a regular basis. When book clubs are first introduced, teachers may sit in on each group—seeing two groups a day, for example—while other students continue to read independently. As students become more proficient at having small-group discussions on their own, they meet for part of each reading workshop, and the teacher visits less frequently.

Both reading and writing are essentially solo acts. There is no doubt that students grow as readers and writers by sharing their thinking and writing or that group work has an important role in literacy learning. But when our students practice reading and writing, they generally do it alone. Mathematics is different. While students definitely need individual time to practice math skills, form theories, and test generalizations, they can do math together and, in fact, gain a great deal from doing so. Mathematics lends itself readily to group work, and the bulk of a day's independent math work may well be spent working with groups or partners.

When my fourth graders are investigating part-to-whole relationships, symmetry, and congruence in our unit on geometry, small groups work together to figure out how many different ways they can arrange four right triangles. Groups are formed randomly; I may pull four slips of paper from a cup containing each student's name. I always set ground rules:

1. Each group member is responsible for his or her own work and behavior (no slacking off or hiding behind more enthusiastic math students).

2. Each member has to help others who ask.

3. Groups can ask the teacher for help only when all members have the same question.

4. All group members should be prepared to share the group's work (to safeguard against the most confident member taking over).

Before starting to work as a group, students have five minutes to work on their own. Some children jump right in, rotating paper triangles and taping them carefully along adjoining sides. Others sit back; they look hesitant but seem curious about what their more confident peers are busy doing (interestingly, some of these reticent kids are very capable when it comes to numbers; they're used to being good at math). Still others arrange and piece together one shape, then sit back and wait to contribute it to the group's efforts.

After five minutes, small groups come together to share their discoveries, questions, and—yes—frustrations. For the rest of the independent work time, they work together, helping each other see when they repeat a shape and challenging each other to discover new ones. They also help each other come up with a system for proving they have indeed found all possible shapes. They cheer each other on.

This kind of group work successfully serves students on all points of the learning spectrum. Students who excel in math get practice explaining their thinking and are often surprised that there are alternative, equally interesting ways to think about things. Students who struggle get scaffolding from their peers—often more effective than adult, professional interventions.

A reminder, however: Group work is not and should not be the only way students work. We need to respect individual students' interests and the need to take a break from the challenges of group work from time to time. I never forget that, at my discretion, I can give certain students permission to work alone when it seems appropriate.

Younger children have more success working with partners than in small groups. Group work is hard, and kindergartners and first graders are still beginning to learn how to share, take turns, and express their thoughts. When my class of kindergartners and first graders is exploring doubles, I am interested (but not surprised) to note that they come up with several different answers for $9 + 9$.

Though young children are definitely interested in adding big numbers like nine, it can be challenging for them to keep track of what they are counting. This is a normal developmental stage. Many five-year-olds are still mastering one-to-one correspondence (counting each object once and only once) and have yet to develop reliable strategies for keeping track of which objects they have counted. Still, I am troubled; it is important that students know that there is one right answer to 9 + 9, and it is not 19 or 17.

I bring up the problem at our next math workshop. "Yesterday when you were figuring out what happened when you doubled numbers, several partners chose the number nine. When I looked at your papers, I noticed something puzzling: some of you found out that when you doubled nine you got seventeen. Some of you got eighteen. And some of you got nineteen. Now, I know that when you add nine plus nine, it will be the same amount every time. What do you think happened?"

This causes quite a buzz. After all, these young children are very attached to their answers—they are strong believers in the results of their experiments, even when they are wrong. They are also just outgrowing their belief in magic ("Couldn't it be different?"). Still, they are in the process of becoming increasingly rational, and they, too, agree that it really should be one answer every time. I give them their task for the day: they are to work with their partner to find out what 9 + 9 really is and prove it on their shared paper. Both partners need to be able to explain their work.

The children dive in, working with diligence and enthusiasm. They huddle over their papers, suggest strategies, experiment, even argue at times. Every child is engaged. The support of a partner means each child has access to the problem and someone to help make sure everything makes sense. In the buzz, I can decipher supportive comments ("Stop, Lucie, you counted that two times." "Let's try tally marks.")

I walk around the room, helping kids resolve procedural problems ("Who gets to do the first set of tally marks?"), talking with kids about their thinking, reteaching and redirecting as needed, and taking notes about what different individuals are doing. I am impressed with the students' motivation to solve this problem. The stakes are higher than just solving another math problem; they are proving what 9 + 9 is! At the same time, I am aware that these papers will not serve as individual assessments. If I want to know what each of my twenty-eight students truly understands, I need to have them work alone. This particular workshop, however, is designed for them to learn about doubles, not to assess their understanding.

When we gather together to discuss what the children have found out, there is a strong feeling that we should be able to say once and for all what 9 + 9 is. Again, not surprisingly, one pair of children has found (and "proved") that 9 + 9 is 19. I know that the final component of this math workshop, the math share, will give us one more opportunity to agree on an answer.

Working in small groups or with partners is very challenging, no matter how old you are, but also very worthwhile. Learners at all ages are dealing not only with the task at hand but with each other's personalities and learning styles. They are practicing how to listen, support, and help one another. You need to think about how to encourage the most hesitant learners to take active roles and how to teach confident students to be aware of their classmates' feelings and differing styles and abilities. I have conversations early in the year about how it affects others to blurt out the answer or comment "That's easy!" I may ask students to watch how a particularly successful group is working. I may deliberately partner defiantly type A personalities together to give their intimidated classmates a break. Overall, giving kids access to each other's thinking, helping them work together, and building a mathematical community via groups is well worth the effort.

Math Shares (Reflection)

Among the many contributions literacy educators have made in recent decades, the regular sharing of student work at the end of a literacy workshop is at the forefront. Regular sharing of student work has many critical purposes:

◆ it moves the day's learning forward by examining how students have made use of it;

◆ it gives students an opportunity to get feedback from their peers (especially useful for young writers); and

◆ it helps reinforce the bonds of their learning community.

In some ways, students are most ripe for learning at this time—they have heard our minilesson and had a chance to put new ideas or strategies to work, and now they can ask classmates for help to clarify confusion, or, flushed with success, they can show each other, for example, just how they used a new revision strategy.

When teachers first began including a share time in their literacy workshops, the author chair was born. At the end of a literacy workshop, this chair, usually more important and grown-up-looking than a typical student chair, was occupied by a student who then read her writing piece. The teacher solicited comments and helped the audience find more to say than simply "I liked your piece" and "You should add more details." Though the author chair had its benefits, it was not as helpful as teachers had hoped it would be. Reading to such a large audience did not always generate constructive feedback. Because sharing remained important, teachers began to invent other ways for students to get feedback.

In *The Writing Workshop*, Katie Wood Ray and Lester Laminack (2001) outline four kinds of *writing shares*:

Four Kinds of Writing Shares

Simple response shares: Partners read to each other and offer one another feedback.

Survey shares: All students share something about the same topic: a line they particularly like, a challenge they are having, a book that has influenced them, and so on. The class then discusses what it notices in the group's responses.

Focused shares: Similar to survey shares, in focus shares small groups or partners share and discuss what they notice.

Student-as-teacher shares: Students teach their classmates something that has been effective for them.

In literacy workshops, students may share how they used a particular comprehension or decoding strategy; read an example from a text that made a particular impression on them as readers; discuss current struggles, goals, or interests; or teach their classmates something that has helped them as a reader (a fourth grader of mine who had struggled to stay focused taught his classmates to place a bookmark a few pages ahead, then read with the goal of reaching it). Teachers play an essential role in planning and leading a share. We want to be sure that at this time we are not just celebrating our students' efforts, but that as a class community, we are learning from them.

In a math workshop, after my students have grappled with the day's math, either on their own or in a group, I gather them together for a brief sharing of their work. This could be as few as five minutes or as long as thirty, depending upon the focus of the share and the limits of our time and energy.

Shares at the conclusion of a math workshop are as diverse as literacy shares. Students may share their solution strategies with a partner and listen to feedback. I may ask all students to share one example of a shape they made that day with pattern block stickers. We then discuss what we notice in the class's examples. I may ask small groups to look at and discuss one solution they came up with for a problem with many possible answers (different ways to get a sum of twenty, for example, or ways to cover a yellow hexagon with other pattern block shapes). I may ask a student who has made good use of an invented subtraction strategy to teach it to her classmates.

Talk is key in math shares. Students' voices should dominate. I want students of all ages talking to their classmates about their mathematical thinking and their strategies. Then, I want their classmates to talk back: to respectfully challenge ideas or strategies, ask for clarification, and add related ideas. I expect students to listen to each other and hold each other accountable. I clearly let students know that they are responsible for hearing *and* understanding each other's ideas. My students know that their responses are welcome, whether it be a request for clarification ("I don't understand."), a restating of what they have heard ("Allegra was saying she thinks the numerator is always smaller than the denominator."), an opinion ("I respectfully disagree with Allegra because there is the fraction three-halves."), or an extension ("I think Allegra is partially right because she is talking about fractions smaller than one whole, and improper fractions are bigger than one whole.").

When I do my very best teaching, I say almost nothing. Instead, I call on students by nodding silently to them. As these extremely rich discussions progress, students stop talking to me and begin to address one another. Of course, it takes time and effort to lay the groundwork for these kinds of classroom conversations. I recommend reading *Classroom Discussions,* by Suzanne Chapin, Catherine O'Connor, and

Nancy Canavan Anderson (2009), for guidance in leading rich classroom talk about mathematics.

Finally, by closing a math workshop with a math share, we set the stage for the next day's work. Teachers may conclude the share with a preview of what is to come in the days ahead, planting the seeds for future learning.

The Whole Picture

Though there is a definite philosophy to workshop teaching, it is not a curriculum. It is a structure amenable to any number of curricula and all topics (it is not hard to imagine a physical education workshop in the same model). It can—and should—look different in the hands of different teachers working in different schools. What is crucial is the focus on instruction, practice, and reflection, with the central idea that students learn best when they are doers, too.

FROM READING TO MATH TO YOUR CLASSROOM

1. *How will you transition to using a math workshop approach?*

2. *What other components of your literacy workshop might be transferable to a math workshop?*

3. *What rules and expectations would you need to have in place in order to have an effective math workshop?*

4. *How can you maintain a good balance of independent and collaborative work in math class?*

5. *How might you conduct math shares in your class?*

Assessment

Have you ever felt that students' scores on assignments and tests were not providing a clear picture of them as mathematicians? Have you wondered how to get a more complete view of their understanding?

Things are not always what they seem. Olga Torres, a teacher of extraordinary gifts, once gave her young students a math problem based on the classic children's book *Rooster's Off to See the World* (Carle 1972). In this beautifully illustrated tale, a rooster rallies his friends to travel, but when night falls—and cold and hunger set in—the animals, group by group, return home. After reading the book and marveling over the story and its wonderful illustrations, Olga asked the children to figure out how many animals "went off to see the world." Most of the children began making drawings, tally marks, and other symbols representing Rooster and his companions. One boy sat dreamily over his paper, then drew a rooster and a *1*. Olga was puzzled—Why had he gotten it wrong? Had he understood the story? Did he know what he was supposed to do? Olga sat by her student and gently asked him how he got his answer. He replied, "Well, I thought it was none, but then I decided it was one."

Olga asked him to say more. "Who was the one?"

"The rooster," said the student. "At first I thought none, because they all went home. And then I decided one, because Rooster *dreamed* he went off to see the world."

Olga was delighted—this young student was right! She had learned, once again, that there is more than one way to get an answer right.

The subject of assessment is as rich and complex as the subject of learning itself. Indeed, in many respects learning and assessment are one and the same, and learning can be seen as a process of ongoing assessment. First, we acquire information or skills. As time passes, we evaluate the validity and sufficiency of the information or usefulness of the skill. If it falls short, we revise our understanding or refine our skill. Learners never stop asking themselves, "What else is there to know? How can I do it better or more efficiently?" Effective teachers never stop asking the same about their students. The practice of assessment, then, is woven into the learning process.

Assessment serves many purposes, from providing informal feedback to students to providing formal feedback to educational authorities at the city, state, and federal levels. In the end, assessment equates to providing information about students (what they know and how they learn) and information about teachers (how success-fully they teach). At its finest, assessment is a genuine, mutual exchange between teacher and student resulting in insight for both. The teacher gains insight that makes her a better teacher, and the student gains insight that results in more learning.

It isn't always this way. We often experience assessment—*the test*—as judgment conferred upon us. "Am I smart? Am I stupid?" When I was a student, these judgments were central to my performance. I was a grade hound; I'd do almost anything to get an A in math. Learning was secondary, at best. Then, when I entered high school, the world seemed to split into two groups: algebra people and geometry people. I was, most decidedly, an algebra person (it mystifies me today why my math teachers chose to separate so completely these intricately entwined strands of mathematics). Algebra made perfect sense to me, and simplifying and solving algebra problems was deeply satisfying. Geometry, on the other hand, befuddled me. My grades, much to my despair, suffered. I am sure my teachers cared, but I do not remember any attempts by teachers to get inside my misunderstanding. What I do remember were tests. And cheating. And passing—but emerging none the wiser (and much the guiltier).

As a teacher, I view the learning process as having the utmost importance; I want my students to value it as highly as I do. Tests and grades, I've decided, do not get to the heart of what I want to know nor help my students learn about themselves. If I want to find out what my students are thinking—what they are succeeding in, what they find challenging, what they delight in, and what they abhor—I need to find out in other ways. My search has led me to discover that there is much in the assessment I do in reading and writing that I can do with young mathematicians.

Parallels in How to Assess Literacy and Mathematics Learning

There is no single practice that is sufficient in accomplishing the many goals of assessment. In the literacy classroom, teachers employ a combination of assessment procedures, including

- conferences (individual interviews),
- running records,
- retellings,
- analysis of student work,
- observation,
- spelling quizzes,
- reader's notebooks and journals, and
- self-assessment.

These assessment procedures have shaped the expectations of literacy learning: they demand that, in order to demonstrate success, students have to be able to do much more than answer comprehension questions or hand in completed writing assignments. These procedures teach students how to reflect on their reading and writing abilities, how to name and select strategies, and how to evaluate the success of their own work. I want my students to develop the same skills and attitudes in math as they do in literacy learning.

No matter what the subject area, assessment is most effective when

- expectations are clearly defined;
- it is conducted on an ongoing basis;

◆ it is used to drive instruction;
◆ it includes analysis of student work, with special attention to miscues as teaching and learning opportunities; and
◆ it involves students and develops the capacities for self-correction and metacognition.

You can carry out effective assessment of mathematics learning by applying the classroom-based assessment strategies that further literacy learning. Let's take an in-depth look at each of the literacy assessment procedures previously listed, this time under a mathematical lens, while simultaneously keeping our focus on the characteristics of effective assessment.

Conferences (Individual Interviews)

In reflecting on my dismal experiences with geometry, I wish my teacher had spent time helping me figure out what was wrong with my reasoning. There must have been some reason I was not making sense of the math she was teaching. Conferring with me, she might have helped me see where my sense making was going astray.

Conferring takes place daily in the literacy class, with the typical goal being to meet with each child once over the course of a week to help him become a better reader or writer. When conferring, teachers sit beside a student and talk one-on-one with her. They have an informal conversation about what the student is currently working on in reading or writing. In *How's It Going?* Carl Anderson (2000) explains how he breaks up writing conferences into two parts: first, "conversation about the work the child is doing as a writer" and then "conversation about how the child can become a better writer":

> In the first part, we talk with students about the work they are doing as writers. By "work" I mean what students are doing as they write in their writers notebooks or compose drafts. Are they trying to decide what kind of writing they're going to do—a poem, a memoir, a list book? Are they trying to put spaces between their words? Are they working on a lead or an ending? Are they revising? Checking for spelling?
> As we talk with students about the work they are doing, our job is to make an assessment of what they are doing as writers in that moment

in time. By listening carefully to their words and by reading their writ-
ing, we gather information about who students are at that moment as
spellers or revisers or editors of their writing. With this information in
mind, we decide what to teach them. (16–17)

Conferring is useful in assessing a host of literacy skills, understandings, and attitudes, including the ability to self-reflect, comprehension, understanding of the writing process, knowledge of genres,
and how comfortable and interested students are in their work. Because
it involves seeing the student right where he is as a reader or writer, and
because it leads so directly and immediately to effective teaching, conferring is a uniquely powerful and exciting assessment procedure.

Conferring also takes some time to master. There are pitfalls:
teachers are often distracted by the piece of writing itself; the conversation becomes focused on suggestions that will improve the writing
piece but not necessarily the writer. At other times teachers have a
tendency to focus on the personal issues raised in a student's writing,
or in the connections the student makes in reading rather than the
work the student is doing as a writer or reader. Even when conferring
does succeed at staying focused on the student's specific reading and
writing work, teachers often find it challenging to accomplish the
dual tasks of assessing *and* teaching.

In order to be effective, conferring requires good questions, good
listening, and a solid understanding of the reading and writing
process. Teachers get better at the skill with practice, reflection, and
study.

Conferring in mathematics follows a similar structure to conferring in literacy: teachers ask questions to find out how a student is
thinking about the math she is doing, then the teacher decides what
to teach based on this assessment. The basic premise of conferring
holds: we try to improve the student, *not* the piece of work she is
doing at the time. Instead of showing a student how to solve a challenging problem (for example, coaxing him through steps that may
stymie him), you should probe his thinking and find out where he
has misconceptions, gaps in understanding, or deficient skills. In the
end, though you'd like to see correct answers, what you really want is
a smarter student. This focus affects how you question and listen.
When I first began conferring in the math class, I examined my
attitudes—instead of looking at students as *right* or *wrong* in any given

situation, I assumed, like Olga, that my students were doing what they could to *make sense* of the math they were doing. My job was to find out where their misunderstandings were and to teach into those.

When I pull my chair up next to Annie, she bristles. Annie is new to our fourth-grade class and unused to conferring. She reminds me of myself; Annie likes to be right and does not like others finding out when she isn't. She is wrestling with a challenging division problem:

> *Four friends found a coin purse with three five-dollar bills, two ones, and a photo of a small dog in their school's playground. When no one came to claim it, the principal gave them permission to share the goods. How much would each child get?*

After ten minutes into the work period, Annie's paper is still blank. She has written and erased *16 ÷ 4 = 4*.

"How are you doing?" I ask her. This is the first part of our conference: what is she doing as a mathematician?

"I don't get it," she confesses. "I don't think it works."

I probe further: "What do you mean? What doesn't work?"

"The problem," she answers. "You can't divide seventeen by four."

I continue my research: "How did you decide to divide seventeen by four?"

"Well," says Annie, "there are three five-dollar bills, so that's five times three. Five times three is fifteen, plus two more is seventeen. And there are four friends. And my teacher last year told me *each* is a keyword for division or multiplication. I decided it had to be division because multiplying would make the numbers too big. But the numbers must be wrong, because you can't divide seventeen by four. Maybe it should be sixteen—should it?" She looks worried and tentative.

Annie's answer is rich in information: First, she knows her way into the problem. She can easily solve 5 × 3. She knows some facts are extraneous (small dog?), and she knows that sixteen is divisible by four. I also learn that she has been taught a *keyword* approach to solving story problems (this is not my preferred strategy, as it often removes students from the context and leads to nonsensical solutions) and that she is either unaware of or uncomfortable with division with remainders. She has not recorded her handy solution to the total amount in the wallet and might need more teaching there. She also lacks confidence in herself as a mathematician and looks to the teacher for answers.

Now I am at the second part of the conference: I need to decide what I will teach in this conference. What will be of most use to Annie now *and* in the future? After all, it would not be too hard to get her to solve this problem correctly. But I want much more than that—I want to arm her with tools to solve future problems. I decide to tackle Annie's discomfort with division with remainders, hoping as a side effect of my teaching that she'll question the keyword approach. I'll emphasize *making sense of the story by connecting it to experience.*

"I guess they could have found sixteen," I say. "But it was seventeen—you figured that out easily." (This is my subtle attempt to boost confidence.) "Are you sure they can't share seventeen dollars? It would be a shame to just leave it there, don't you think, after they were so honest and really tried to find the owner? *What would you do?* Would you just give it back, or make it sixteen?"

Annie looks puzzled for a moment. "No . . . ," she says slowly. The wheels seem to be turning.

"Think out loud," I coax, "so I can hear what you're thinking."

"Well," Annie continues, "I guess I'd try to share it all. I guess we could each have four dollars, and then we'd have a dollar left over." She looks at me, expectantly.

"Yes?" I ask, sending the ball back to her court. Bing! I can practically see the lightbulb go off. "Don't tell me!" I smile. "I think you know what to do now."

I leave Annie hard at work. Confident she has a plan up her sleeve, I want her to work independently. Even if she doesn't get a right answer, she knows a little more about the kind of problem she is doing. I am curious to see what she'll come up with on her own. This conference lasts less than ten minutes—time well spent.

The Role of Questioning in Conferring
The way you word a question is integral to your communication in conferences. Students can be gifted at sensing teachers' underlying motives and can end up providing answers that they know the teacher wants to hear rather than answers that are true to their thoughts and understanding. Especially avoid questions that lead students to think of what might be right or wrong in the way they answer. In conferring

on mathematics, I've learned to ask open-ended questions like "What's up?" or "How are you doing?" When a teacher asks a student a leading question such as "Are you sure this answer is right?" he is usually signaling that the answer is wrong. Generally such a question is actually a statement: "This answer is wrong—try again." Very little is accomplished with this type of question: basically, the child learns she has messed up. When the teacher asks, on the other hand, "How do you know this answer is right?" *whether the answer is correct or not*, he is likely to learn an enormous amount about how a student thinks. It is clear that a child who says, "Because I lined the numbers up carefully," thinks very differently from the child who answers, "I know that ten more than twenty-one is thirty-one and three more makes thirty-four." You can accomplish much more with open-ended questions: You'll learn more about how the child thinks and be able to make a nuanced decision about what to teach the child next. In the meantime, the child has learned that you value her thinking.

Open-ended questioning often requires a shift in teachers' thinking and attitudes. It is discomfiting for us to see students make the same errors repeatedly; hence, we tend to want to point out the clear nonsense of their answers. However, students learn very little by having their errors pointed out to them again and again. Helpful conferring questions encourage answers that give insights into the kind of sense the student is trying to make. These questions include the following:

Key Conferring Questions

How did you figure that out?
How does this make sense to you?
Why did you decide to do it this way?
How can you be sure this is correct?

The questioning and listening that happens in conferring express our caring and commitment to a child's learning. I was concerned with Annie's developing understanding of division, but I was also worried about her lack of confidence and discomfort with wrong answers. My questions encompassed both.

Finally, conferring can effectively drive classroom instruction. When teachers observe different students struggling with the same issues in conference after conference, they can tailor whole-class lessons to meet the widespread need. These lessons can take place any time—during the share session, on a following day, or even midlesson.

Running Records

Reading is ephemeral; unlike writing, even when we hear a student read aloud, we have no record of what the student did, making reading all the more difficult to assess. This is where running records come to the rescue. Running records were devised as a technique for recording and analyzing a student's oral reading. To take a running record, teachers listen to a student read a text and use an established technique to track the student's successful reading as well as misread words, reread words, omitted words, and self-corrections. Running records allow teachers to observe and record just what the student is doing as a reader. Teachers may prompt students to have a go at words they are stuck on or coax them to keep going; however, running records differ from conferring in that they are not a conversation. Running records reveal students' strategies for decoding, fluency, reading level, and attention to comprehension.

Teachers use the data collected in running records to analyze students' mistakes (or miscues), calculate accuracy rates from the quantity and type of errors, and determine which decoding strategies students favor and which ones they need to learn. Running records are incredibly compatible with leveled libraries; together they help ensure students are reading at a just-right level. Because these records provide so much information about how readers are figuring out unfamiliar words, they're taken primarily on students who are still mastering decoding.

Early childhood teachers were the first to embrace running records. (At last! A tool for getting inside those fascinating, puzzling young minds.) It was soon clear that a similar tool was needed to understand our youngest math students. While older kids can be extremely eloquent about their thinking processes, young students are decidedly not. When asked, "How did you get that answer?" they are likely to answer something along the lines of "I did it with my brain." (In addition, number concepts, such as place value, are so abstract that it is almost impossible for young students to verbalize an understanding of them.) Just as teachers learn about early reading by observing and recording early reading behavior, we can observe and record early math behavior.

For example, counting is a critical skill in mathematics. Although the simple counting of whole numbers is one of our first mathematical accomplishments, we are introduced to increasingly sophisticated ways to count throughout our education. Rote counting—that is, simply knowing the counting sequence—is easy to assess. But it is soon insufficient, and we need to know if kids are linking the words they are chanting to quantities. The way we do this is by watching young kids count.

When I was curious about one of my first graders, Avivah, and her ability to count, I equiped myself with a cup of Unifix cubes and took her to a quiet corner of the room (I had asked her to do some math with me so I could get to know her better as a learner). I hoped to learn four things in observing Avivah's activities:

◆ how well she could chant the counting sequence;

◆ whether she could relate that counting to real objects;

◆ if she had a method for keeping track of the objects she counted; and

◆ if she knew the difference between cardinal and ordinal numbers.

I sat down with Avivah and immediately asked her, "How high can you count?" Avivah was a bright and confident girl, eager to please and exceptionally tolerant of the noisy kids in the block area. She counted with ease in a charming singsong, pausing at each count of ten as if she were waiting for the word to float into her mind, "Twenty-eight, twenty-nine . . . thirty!" I took notes as she counted, adding ellipses to indicate her pauses (I would refer to these notes later when planning small-group work in math). Going strong, Avivah finished with a triumphant "Ninety-nine, one hundred!"

I smiled and asked, "What comes next?"

Avivah replied with a pause and a cautious "Two hundred?"

"Thanks, Avivah," I responded. As with conferring, the wording is so important. I didn't want to convey whether Avivah was right or wrong—after all, because this was assessing, not teaching, her answers couldn't really be wrong. Her continued willingness to let me in on her thinking was critical to this process. On the other hand, two hundred definitely does not come right after one hundred; we'd have to work on that at a later time.

Satisfied that Avivah had a great handle on first-grade rote counting by ones, I now wanted to see how she counted things. Handing her a cup of twenty-four cubes, I asked her to count them. Avivah proved to be an excellent counter of things: Pouring them into a neat pile, she began counting smoothly, tagging a cube with a spoken number and dragging it into another, quickly growing pile. When the two piles threatened to merge, she paused in her counting, separated them, and continued where she left off. "Twenty-four!" she exclaimed. I took note again of her confidence and her enthusiasm.

I pulled a smaller group of cubes aside and lined them up. "How many now?" I asked. Avivah gazed intently at the row of nine cubes. "Nine," she said.

"Wow!" I responded. "Can you do that out loud now, so I can hear?"

Avivah complied patiently, again tagging while counting, though this time she did not move the cubes.

I followed up with two questions: "Can you show me two?" Avivah pulled the first two slightly away from the rest. "And can you show me the fifth?"

After a moment of thought, Avivah pointed to the fifth in the line and said: "This one!"

I finished our interview by thanking Avivah again. I had learned a lot about this capable young math student, and I let her know it.

Naturally, not all of my students are as confident or capable as Avivah. By making numbers or quantities larger or smaller and asking follow-up questions, I can adapt the assessment to better probe different children's thinking. In this way, like a running record, the assessment is constructed to show what a child can do without putting her in a situation of repeated failure.

I avoided failure with Thomas when I suspected that he was strug-gling with our daily math activities and had trouble keeping track of twenty-four objects. In his running record, I planned to start him with a smaller amount and increase the number if he was successful. Yet another example was Antonio, who was still learning English and was experiencing increased difficulty with the counting sequence. Though I am only a beginning speaker of Spanish, I offered him the opportunity to count in his native language. This allowed me to focus on his mathematical skills instead of his ability to speak English. It is a careful balance: we must offer activities that allow us to see where kids need more instruction and practice without undermining their developing confidence.

Retellings

In the simple yet powerful assessment procedure called *retelling*, stu-dents retell stories they have read, either orally or in writing. While retelling was originally used as a reading strategy for helping students stay engaged, teachers who have had students do regular retellings have seen additional benefits: students develop a better understand-ing of various literary genres, increase their vocabularies, exercise many literacy activities, and become motivated to reread texts. Most importantly, retelling serves as an excellent assessment procedure, telling teachers volumes about students' comprehension, their ability to use the language, and the suitability of the texts they are reading.

In the mathematics class, students engage in a form of retelling when they communicate their mathematical interpretations, both orally and in writing. As a general practice, when I ask my students questions like "How did you get that answer?" "How do you define even and odd numbers?" or "Can you think of another way to solve that?" I am initiating a powerful assessment and learning process.

In *Classroom Discussions,* Chapin, O'Connor, and Anderson write:

> *We've all experienced learning about a concept by listening to a teacher talk about it. After we listen to the teacher we may feel we understand the concept. However, when asked to put the concept into words, we may discover that our understanding is not as deep as we thought. We may become inarticulate, even speechless. We don't yet have the under-standing necessary to put the idea into words. Yet unless we are put in*

a situation where we must talk or write clearly about the concept, we
may never come to realize that our knowledge is insufficient. (2009, 7)

Mathematical retellings take several forms: students may write
about their thinking processes, explain them aloud, or retell others'
thinking processes. Whether my students talk or write, I learn about
their misconceptions, strategies for computation, understanding of
concepts, reasoning abilities, and attitudes and confidence.

Students who are explaining their thinking aloud have three
audiences: their teachers, their classmates, and themselves. When we
expect that solution strategies will make sense, any of those listening
audiences can point out when thinking is unclear and support students
in making their explanations clearer. This is especially useful—and
powerful—when the one who notices errors is the student himself,
pausing midexplanation to say, "No, wait; that's not right."

In order to get this kind of honesty, you need to create a classroom
that feels safe to all your students. Because your students are still
learning respect and empathy, you need to address and readdress
respectful behavior often. When children act disrespectfully to each
other, I am quick to stop it. When a fourth grader makes an obvious
mistake, for example, a few of his classmates start laughing, giving
each other *How dumb can you be?* looks. "Wait—hold everything!" I
silence the laughter. There is no mistaking the serious look on my face
and the tone of my voice. "Nick is taking a risk with his thinking here,
and he can't do that if people are going to laugh." My fourth graders
looked around uneasily. Nick is looking pretty uneasy, too.

"Go ahead, Nick," I continue. Nick nods and repeats his faulty
conjecture. This time, no matter how wrong his classmates think he
is, no one laughs. Instead, they quietly raise their hands. I call on
Sara, banking on her sensitivity and ability to ask good questions. In
the end, Nick finds the flaw in his thinking. The message is clear; his
attempt and Sara's respectful questioning hold more value than a
quick, right answer.

Analysis of Student Work

In reading classes, teachers review reading logs and students' writing
to better understand each student's range and volume of reading,

familiarity with different genres, and reading comprehension. In writing classes, teachers look at students' work in writer's notebooks, published pieces, and drafts. Making this type of assessment tells teachers not what students *can do* but what they *actually do* in reading and writing.

In literacy, simple tools like reading logs reveal when there's a problem. When a student records that she has read from page 10 to page 20 in her daily thirty minutes of home reading, the teacher knows something is up; ten pages is very few for thirty minutes of reading. The student is either reading extremely slowly, reading a book that is much too hard, or reading for a lot less than thirty minutes. It is also quite unusual for readers to read from one multiple of ten to another (Are students so disengaged from reading that they pick a goal—in this case, from page 10 to page 20—hold their noses, and read simply to fulfill the assignment? Are such log entries fictional altogether?).

Readers also write about the books they are reading. Whether it is on sticky notes or in longer compositions, this writing tells a lot about the specific comprehension strategies students are (or are not) using and how successfully they are being applied. Are students paying attention to more than the plot? Do they take note of their own connections, reactions, and confusion? Do they relate the text to the other books they have read? Do they attend to a character's development?

Teachers who assess writers by looking at their written work at all steps of the writing process—from the informal gathering of ideas in the writer's notebook to the drafting, revising, and editing stages—have extremely rich material from which to learn about their students. In fact, these days teachers are stocking their classrooms with eraserless pencils and ballpoint pens so they can see the errors, omissions, and revisions the eraser so often conceals.

By considering the writer at all stages of the process, teachers see so much more than by solely looking at a final draft or published piece. For one, teachers can feel more confident that they are looking at their students' efforts rather than the duplicated efforts of a parent, friend, or even the Internet. Teachers also see how adeptly students apply revision strategies, how accurate initial spellings are, and where students get their ideas.

The information teachers gather in reviewing students' writing (including the writing about their reading) helps them with particular students' needs as well as in forming guided reading and writing groups and making decisions about whole-class instruction.

Analyzing student work is also critical in teaching mathematics. Students are often quite accomplished in restating procedures and strategies that they do not actually use, hence making it critical that teachers look at how students actually *do* mathematics.

The process of gathering written examples of students' mathematical thinking is not as direct as gathering writing is in literacy—after all, a lot of mathematical thinking happens in our heads. In addition, math is often best learned with the use of manipulatives or through games; such materials leave a poor record for study. In order to collect student work for analysis, I practice giving students written prompts and guidelines for completing them. For example, when my primary students are learning early addition, I ask them to solve a basic problem (8 + 7) and write about how they figured it out. For my older students, I learn how they are thinking about fractions by asking them to write about this question: *True or false? Two-fifths is greater than* $\frac{3}{8}$. *Explain.*

Students need practice and instruction in how to record their mathematical thinking. There are often discrepancies between how children solve a problem (whether in their heads or on their fingers) and the solution strategies they record. Sometimes it is too difficult for them to capture and convey the mental sequence they go through; other times they are simply more interested in a peer's solution strategy and prefer recording that. There is no simple answer to this problem; after all, children are learning when they look at each other's work. Instead of simply condemning copying, we need to teach them the difference between *copying* and *drawing inspiration* from one another. I often talk about this distinction with students.

"Sometimes it is hard to write or draw how we solve problems," I say. "Sometimes you might be interested in trying another person's way. When I look at your math paper, we will talk about whether you recorded the way you did it or you tried another way." No matter how young or old my students are, I know I need to model many possible strategies, including drawing fingers and writing *I know that fact by heart.*

One benefit of analyzing a set of student papers is that, though they always bear the stamp of the students' personalities, they can be studied at leisure with a trusted fellow teacher, who can help see past preconceptions. There are times when my colleague can see the sense in a student's paper, whereas I just see the student struggling.

Sitting with my colleague Jennifer Purdy, I pull out Colin's paper. I have asked my first graders to solve 9 + 6. "Ugh. It's just a mess," I say, looking at Colin's scrawls. "He still doesn't get it."

"No, wait a minute—look at this," Jennifer stops me. I look where she is pointing. Sure enough, what initially looked like scribbles do in fact seem to be tally marks. I count them up—fifteen. And they are arranged in two rows. There are still other scribbles and scrawls that are undecipherable—what are they about? Jennifer's thoughtful examination of Colin's paper makes me rethink my preconceptions. Clearly there is more going on than I am giving Colin credit for. Maybe the scribbles mean more, too. I make a plan to inquire further with Colin about what he has drawn.

Observation

Our preconceptions don't just affect the way we look at an individual student's work; they can color our impressions of a whole class. Just as it is crucial to take the time to look critically (and fairly) at student work, it makes sense to give this same attention to how the whole class functions. This is where observation comes into play.

By observing the whole literacy class, teachers take note of students' reading and writing stamina, reading and writing attitudes, and other behaviors. For example, some students engage in a whole lot of reading and writing activities and get precious little done. These students spend a disproportionate amount of workshop time selecting books, sharpening pencils, looking up words in the dictionary, or chatting with a partner. Although teachers are usually aware which students have difficulty focusing, direct and sustained observation either confirms these suspicions or yields the pleasant surprise that active students *are* actively getting work done. Observing these behaviors in math class is equally enlightening.

Observation takes discipline. As teachers, we often have a hard time withdrawing from the ongoing management of the classroom to observe. For example, noise plays a controversial role in the classroom. Though it is widely accepted that students do benefit from talking about their thinking, a noisy classroom is often unnerving to teachers, who cannot shake the sense that all that noise is unproductive. However, when I sit back and observe noisy math classrooms at work, I am often surprised to see how on task students are. This is not to say that noisy classrooms aren't sometimes too noisy and require heightened management; when students (or you) have trouble concentrating, the classroom *is* too noisy. But it is eye-opening to step back from your need to manage and observe the productivity in a noisy classroom.

Observation can help you assess your own management, routines, and seating decisions. Are students getting to work quickly with the supplies they need? Do they have routines for solving their dilemmas and answering their questions without constantly coming to you? Are students seated in productive groups? On the average day, classrooms should run smoothly without constant teacher intervention, and taking time out to observe helps confirm whether this is happening.

Fact Mastery

Spelling and fact quizzes have long been features of school life. They are often the most direct way to find out if students know a certain group of words or set of math facts. And just as there have always been students who succeed in quizzes and those who don't, there have always been teachers who like quizzes and those who don't.

For those of us who dislike quizzes, two problems are apparent: First, quizzes often fail to accurately assess spelling and fact knowledge. There are students who routinely fail such quizzes but are competent at the regular work. Second, there is frequently poor transference of mastery. I am troubled to see students succeed in stand-alone spelling or fact quizzes, then go on to routinely misspell spelling words and make minor calculation errors in their daily writing and math work.

Teachers are rightly convinced that students must learn to spell conventionally in order to write fluidly and intelligibly. Similarly, speedy recall of basic math facts is absolutely necessary in doing higher-level mathematics. Thus quizzes remain quick, simple, and—to a degree—motivating. What we need to focus on, however, is the assessment potential of quiz taking.

Teachers have moved away from assigning random spelling-word lists and instead use thematic lists. Such lists test students' abilities to spell words that reveal mastery of various spelling patterns as well as sight-word knowledge. Teachers then analyze student errors to make curriculum choices and create word study groups for further instruction. Students also favor these thematic lists; by looking at their own work, they find out just what it is about spelling that is challenging to them.

In mathematics, teachers continually try to refine the time-honored tradition of timed quizzes to make them more useful for students. To successfully do so, we need to clearly define *fact mastery*. Suzanne Chapin and Art Johnson write that "*mastery* does not imply that students are human calculators able to perform at lightning speed. It means that they know the facts well enough to be efficient and accurate in other calculations" (2006, 43). Familiarity is essential; automatic recall is not. After all, students (and adults) can be quite effective mathematicians even when they need more than a second to recall such facts as 7×8. (A good rule of thumb is that students should be able to come up with a basic fact within three to five seconds.)

Teachers are also starting to give more time for students to memorize facts. For example, in many schools, including the ones where I teach, mastery of multiplication facts has been moved from third to fourth grade. Teachers agree that emphasizing a solid conceptual understanding of multiplication (including skip-counting, grouping, and area models) results in better overall computational ability and makes fact mastery easier.

Teachers and students also spend more time analyzing just how many facts there are to work on. When my fourth graders begin the process of memorizing multiplication facts, we start by looking carefully at the times table. When the complete table is laid before them, it is daunting. It has 144 multiplication pairs! Upon closer examination, however, students realize that some of the facts are extremely easy. After all, you don't need to memorize the ones, and twos are

doubles—most kids have those internalized before they start studying multiplication. And the tens? They're the quick ones. My students
often get squares next. Elevens have a cool pattern, easily learned.
And the commutative property, once it is understood, cuts the
remaining number of multiplication pairs in half, leaving fewer than
thirty! Not bad, especially as some of these are fives, also quickly mastered. The job is suddenly a lot less daunting.

After this reassuring analysis, I begin giving students quizzes,
starting with simple quizzes comprising the ones, twos, tens, and
elevens. Before I expect them to show what they know about the
more complex facts, I want them to be comfortable taking quizzes.
Once students are familiar and comfortable with the quiz process, I
begin emphasizing the complex facts. Allowing three to four seconds
a fact, I expect students to complete forty-eight problems in three
minutes (or thirty-two in two minutes).

"Before we get started," I coach my students, "remind yourself not
to get stuck on ones you don't remember. Skip those; if you have time
you can go back." (This is unbelievably hard for some students. I
make a habit of sitting by those children and helping them move on
if they get stuck.) There is one final step before starting: in an effort
to relieve the inevitable anxiety some kids feel around testing, I give
them a few minutes to jot their feelings, concerns, and hopes on the
back of the quiz sheet. *I'm nervous,* some write, or *I like quizzes. I think
I will get them all right.*

While the kids are taking the quiz, I observe them at work: Who
is flying through the list? Who is stuck? Who has skipped facts he or
she doesn't know? Who is surprising me? After all, I rarely expect
Dylan to do so well—he generally struggles in math. But he finished
in no time, with accuracy. It's great to see that I'm tapping his strength
for a change! And what's up with Miranda? She is such an insightful
math student, usually so quick with an answer, yet she is frozen over
her paper. I'll have to check in with her later.

"You have used half your time," I finally say. Then, "You have thirty
seconds." At last, "Time's up. Put down your pens. Now take the next
few minutes, and using your colored pencil, work on the ones you
didn't get." I want to give kids a chance to show what they know, even
if it takes more time. As closure, students revisit the writing they did
on the back of their paper before the test. How are they feeling now?

I did great! some students write. And sometimes, *Horrible! I am so bad at this.*

Our next steps are critical. First, I look at the class's work as a whole. If most kids are struggling with nines, for example, I can plan a lesson to help them see the patterns in these multiples. Next, students analyze their own quizzes to figure out which facts they did not get and write a plan for memorizing them. These plans include breaking the times table into manageable chunks, playing games that provide practice, devising shortcuts (*If 9 × 10 is 90, 9 × 9 is 9 less than 90, which equals 81*), and writing mnemonics.

Finally, I check in with the students who are having the most problems. Dylan deserves a big pat on the back; his facility for memorizing facts was a way to build his overall confidence in mathematics. Then on to Miranda. A conversation with her uncovers her sheer terror of tests. A quick (but relaxed) interview reveals that, as I expected, she did know her facts quite well. A quiz is definitely not the best way to assess her understanding. I'll have to quiz her orally. In the meantime, we'll work on relieving her test anxiety.

In the end, I've done my most accurate assessment of students' familiarity with basic facts by observing them at work or listening to them talk about the math. After all, it is the daily, contextual use of facts that counts. The benefits of the quiz are twofold: it puts mastery up front for students and me and results in a written document that both of us can study.

Notebooks and Journals: Writing About Process

Third-, fourth-, and fifth-grade teachers have the fortune, in contrast to their primary-grade colleagues, of getting insights into their students' thinking by asking them to write down their thoughts. The results are deeply illuminating.

In literacy classes, students not only write about the books they are reading but also write about the reading process; the literary genres they are studying; and their own interests, feelings, and attitudes. Reader's notebooks support self-assessment by providing students with an avenue to articulate their thinking. In turn these notebooks become written records for teachers to analyze. Students may write about any aspect of reading—when and where they read best, favorite genres, least favorite genres, or what they find challenging. One struggling reader wrote, in reflecting on the goal of reading twenty-five books over the course of the year: *I feel like I have to read so many books I can't take time to enjoy the one I really want to read. Can we talk about this?*

In the math class, teachers can ask students to write about their mathematical thinking beyond the realm of specific problems. Students may write about their attitudes, preferences, strengths, and challenges. Students might find it helpful to write about the anxiety that accompanies the assessment of multiplication facts. Teachers may ask students to write whether a particular math activity was too hard, too easy, or just right—and to explain why. This kind of writing fosters habits of mind that encourage ongoing self-assessment of math skills, which may well be the most influential form of assessment.

Self-Assessment

Self-assessment has long been an important aspect of literacy classes. Taking a variety of forms, including periodic goal setting and writing self-portraits, self-assessment gives students an active role in their learning. It also provides teachers with a fascinating window into students' thinking: students reveal their understanding of what good reading and writing is, as well as their beliefs in their own competency. Attitudes shine through, as do preferences. Students are often achingly honest, and many are tougher critics than their teachers. Best of all, self-assessment supports students in setting their own goals. Teachers have found this kind of ownership to be exceptionally motivating.

Effective teachers have big goals: they hope to foster independent learners who have the drive and capacity to learn throughout their lifetimes. This is not possible when teachers own assessment: unless students are involved in their assessment, they will not develop the ability to see where they need to seek out more support, practice, or information.

Students who are involved in their own assessment have a better shot at reaching high standards of achievement than those who rely on their teachers' evaluations. This holds true in very concrete examples as well as more complex ones. Again, this begins with knowing where correctness lives (it is not in the teacher). When a student turns to me to confirm an arithmetic answer ("Does seven times eight equal fifty-four?"), I turn the question back to him ("What do you think? How would you prove that seven times eight equals fifty-four?").

In order to self-assess, students need to take four key actions:

◆ *Define success:* Students need to know criteria for success in order to show what they know.

◆ *Find and correct their own errors:* Students need to develop and practice strategies for double-checking their work.

◆ *Reflect:* Students need to reflect on what they have done, taking into consideration both what they know about themselves so far and the criteria for success.

◆ *Plan to do better next time:* This last is especially critical. By holding students responsible for their own growth, teachers make self-assessment more than a thoughtful exercise—it is an active part of the learning cycle.

In addition, to support students' self-assessment, we need to make sure our expectations are clear.

When my fifth graders work on solving complex, multistep problems, many struggle with clear and thorough explanations of their thinking, even when they can get right answers. I'm always curious: Do they know what a good solution should look like? I post a strong solution for my students to analyze (I usually get the example from a colleague's class and make sure the student's name is not on it). We talk about what makes the solution a good one. "It is organized," students point out. "You can tell what she did first and then what she did next. The answer is labeled. It is neat."

After we list the qualities of the example, I give students their work again. "Using another color of pencil," I tell them, "fix yours up. Give your paper these good qualities. Then write me a message: What did you need to fix? What are you already good at, and what do you need to work on?" The results are impressive—and lasting. Knowing what to aim for, and what to work on, gives my students power and responsibility for their own learning.

Similarities in What to Assess in Literacy and Mathematics Learning

Current practices in literacy instruction assess a wide range of information, creating a complete picture of students as readers and writers. Likewise, mathematics assessment must be concerned with much more than computational efficiency. I want a complete picture of my students as mathematicians: their understandings, attitudes, interests, and skills. The following table highlights the similarities in what we assess in literacy and mathematics learning:

Similarities in Literacy and Mathematics Learning Assessments

WHAT IS ASSESSED IN LITERACY	WHAT IS ASSESSED IN MATHEMATICS
attitudes toward reading and writing	attitudes toward mathematics
letter recognition and corresponding sounds	number recognition and corresponding quantities
decoding skills and fluency of use	computational skills and fluency of use
critical thinking: ability to predict, infer, interpret, and relate to own experiences	critical thinking: ability to estimate, evaluate reasonableness of answers, understand in context, and relate to own experiences
content knowledge: text structures, vocabulary, genres of writing, spelling	content knowledge: concepts in the different strands of mathematics, vocabulary, facts
interests and range of reading	interests and preferences in mathematics

Select assessment procedures based on what you want to know. For example, if I am interested in finding out if my students have mastered basic facts and can recall them within a few seconds, I may decide that a quiz may be useful. Or, if I want to know if my students understand the associative property in multiplication, I may ask them to write about the question *Does 4 × 3 equal 3 × 4? Explain why or why not.* If I want to find out why a particular student never completes a day's assignment, I observe and then confer with him. And if I have overall concerns about a student, I do a more formalized, one-on-one assessment interview.

The content and skills involved in literacy and mathematics are naturally quite different. Success in reading and writing means becoming increasingly sophisticated in a few skills: decoding, comprehending, composing, and spelling. Literacy content knowledge lies largely in the different genres; there is a lot to know about poetry, for example. Success in mathematics, on the other hand, requires the mastery of many, many skills and involves very extensive content knowledge.

As a result, you'll probably find yourself using some assessment procedures more frequently in literacy and others more frequently in mathematics. For example, conferring with a student about his daily reading or writing is extraordinarily useful to me. The information gathered through this informal conversation can immediately help students become more sophisticated readers and writers. However, in teaching mathematics, though I find that these conversations are definitely useful, they are not as central to my mathematics instruction as written assessments.

The Whole Picture

Assessment takes place throughout the teaching and learning process. Effective assessment adds to the learning cycle: teachers use what they learn to improve their teaching and make feedback available to students so they can improve their learning. Assessment happens at the beginning of a unit, as it progresses, and at its end. It takes place, in some way, every day.

You can use the assessment procedures that have been discussed in this chapter periodically, on an ongoing basis, or as a summative evaluation. In addition, both you and your students can develop habits of mind that result in constant, ongoing assessment—on the student's part, a belief that math should make sense, and on your part, a belief that students' efforts make sense. The following table summarizes examples of when assessment can be used (see page 120).

Types of Assessment

WHEN	TEACHER INITIATED	STUDENT INITIATED
periodic	standardized assessments formalized assessment tools teacher-devised quizzes	self-analysis goal setting
ongoing	one-on-one interviews conferring notes analysis of student work authentic tasks with opportunities for revision	writing about work peer critiques classroom discussions
assessment habits of mind developed for continual use	error analysis questioning and listening	self-correction and sense making

Teachers' goals in mathematics are shifting. Where once computational efficiency and fact mastery reigned supreme, teachers are now expecting students to be accomplished in more than this. We want students to think of mathematics as a rich and complex realm of relationships, logic, and reasoning. We convey this belief in the way we assess. When you make talking and writing a daily practice, use periodic timed quizzes to support student self-assessment, and seek to understand puzzling students with one-on-one interviews instead of standardized tests, you are conveying a belief that mathematics is a sense-making activity and that students play a powerful role in their learning of it.

FROM READING TO MATH TO YOUR CLASSROOM

1. *Have you ever tried conferring with students about math? How did it go? How could it have gone better?*

2. *How can you help students self-assess their math learning, and what do you want them to focus on when assessing themselves?*

3. *What do you consider to be fact mastery?*

4. *How can you help students define success in different stages of their math learning?*

Supporting Struggling Learners

Have you had certain students who for one reason or another just seemed completely stymied when it came to math? Have you felt equally stymied about how to help them move forward?

R esearch on how to help all children become readers and writers also informs us of how to help children who struggle in mathematics. The suggestions emerging from recent research in literacy do not amount to a reading program. They are not a curriculum. Nor do they advocate a single, specific way to teach reading. Some conclusions amount to driving principles, others to concrete recommendations. Each one of these literacy principles and recommendations applies to the teaching and learning of mathematics:

◆ Reading and writing are thinking, not just the performance of skills.

◆ Reading and writing should be rewarding.

◆ Prior knowledge plays a critical role in successful reading and writing.

◆ Struggling students (and their nonstruggling classmates) need modeling and demonstration of reading and writing skills and strategies.

◆ Fluency is essential to both reading and writing.

◆ Learners benefit enormously from early print experiences, whether at home or in a preschool setting.

◆ Children need to read and write about real things and need to see adults read and write about real things, too.

◆ Children need to read lots of "easy" text to build fluency and comprehension.

◆ There is no one best way to teach reading and writing. The subjects—not to mention the students and their teachers—are simply too complex to be reduced to one approach. Struggling learners need teaching that incorporates aspects of all approaches to teaching literacy.

◆ It takes time to teach and learn reading and writing. Struggling students in particular need time *at school* to read and write. Teachers need dedicated blocks of time to teach reading and writing and students need time to practice them.

◆ Struggling students need expert teachers. Professional development is critical to teaching all students.

◆ Involving families helps struggling students.

Underlying the practical recommendations of educators like Patricia Cunningham, Richard Allington, and Margaret Mooney is a core educational belief: we *can* help all children become readers and writers. This is important: If we believe that some learners simply cannot get it, we have little incentive to hold ourselves responsible and to keep looking for better practices. If we assume some students will inevitably fail, we ensure that they will. On the other hand, when we assume all students can succeed in becoming readers and writers, we don't stop trying. The same holds true for mathematics.

The reality is that though we definitely can help all children become readers and writers, we cannot help them all become the same kind of reader or writer. It is reasonable to hold the belief that all children will become readers and writers; it is not reasonable to expect that all will grow up to become avid readers of literary criticism or writers on the order of Jane Austen or Stephen King. Likewise, I believe we can expect that all children will learn to understand mathematics. Some will move on to become astrophysicists, engineers, theoretical mathematicians, and teachers of mathematics. Most, however, will become adept users of everyday mathematics, able to read and understand statistical information and graphs, compute quantities easily and accurately, think about spatial relations, observe and make use of patterns, and think logically. As an elementary school teacher, it is my responsibility to help all children develop a positive attitude toward the mathematics we are learning and the confidence that they can tackle it. It is also my responsibility to seek out approaches that engage them, enable them, and get all of them ready for the mathematics they will begin learning in middle school and beyond. Some will do it easily and with gusto (in fact, I will need to give them additional mathematics to explore). Others will need much more support and professional problem solving on my part.

Over the years, like all teachers, I have had students who required special attention. This chapter focuses on three such children: Ellie, Artie, and Marshall. Each of these children faced different challenges, and each needed his or her own unique interventions to support his or her growth as a young mathematician. What these three children had in common, beside their difficulties with math, was their seriously damaged self-esteem. They had "failed" so often that they had developed negative identities, attitudes, and expectations about mathematics. Without intervention, their prospects were pretty poor: the further behind they fell, the harder a time they would have grasping the ever more complex math they would be expected to learn. The work educators have done in literacy helped me help Ellie, Artie, and Marshall succeed—each in her or his own way—in understanding and doing mathematics. It helped me set up a classroom environment that supported all students and provided ways to think about reaching each child. Before looking at how we can help children like these one-on-one, let's first think about what we can do to the classroom environment as a whole to provide support.

Creating a Classroom Environment
That Supports All Students

Whether I am teaching kindergarten or fifth grade, I know that the classroom environment I establish is critical to the success of *all* my students, as I discussed in Chapter 4. Knowing that success in learning is highly correlated with experiences that occur *before* formal schooling begins, I take care to make sure I am providing real-life experiences in the class for students who may have missed them. When thinking about how to incorporate informal math experiences into the daily life of the classroom, I ask myself, "What kind of mathematics do parents do with their children at home?" I try to incorporate math talk throughout the day: noticing and marveling at patterns; counting out supplies by ones, fives, and tens; and describing the shapes of things around the room. As I get to know my students, I can focus this talk on those who seem to need it most. The kids who have the least sense that the school math we are doing is a part of their daily lives need to hear me talk about *how* we are making groups of six, for example ("We are splitting the class into fifths.").

Next, I think about scheduling. Just as it takes time to teach and learn literacy, it takes time to teach and learn mathematics. My struggling students need a solid hour or more each day to explore concepts and practice skills, and they need math lessons in the mornings, at least a couple of times a week, when they have the most energy (I am fortunate to be in a school where I have flexibility in my scheduling). See Chapter 4 for more on this topic.

Knowing that struggling readers and writers benefit from doing *real* reading and writing, I make sure that my struggling students are doing plenty of real math. Mathematics educators Cathy Fosnot and Maarten Dolk (2001) have written at length about the importance of helping students *mathematize* the world they live in and think about the mathematics of their experiences. Though I rely largely on a published math curriculum, I've made an effort to provide a real-life context when one is not provided.

For example, the *Investigations in Number, Data, and Space* curriculum developed by TERC provides a compelling context— brownies—for thinking about fractions (in the third-grade unit *Fair*

Shares [Tierney and Berle-Carman 1998]). The first fourth-grade fractions unit, *Different Shapes, Equal Pieces* (Tierney et al. 1998), moves from cakes to geoboards—an abstraction that some of my struggling fourth graders have trouble with. (Asked to divide the geoboard into equal eighths, for example, they can make eight parts but lose sight of making sure the parts are of equal sizes.) Providing context is especially helpful to struggling students: whether it be brownies, pizza, or gold, telling these kids they will be sharing the eight pieces with seven other people—and that the others will choose before they do—provides an incentive, albeit imaginary, for thinking about how to fairly divide the whole.

Struggling students also need ample modeling and instruction. I make modeling and demonstrating a regular part of my lessons. When the day's activities call for the use of a particular material, such as geoboards, pattern blocks, or rulers, I make sure to model the tool before students use it. When the activity does not specify a tool, I use a variety of tools that either illuminate the concepts (for example, for lessons on symmetry, I use leaves) or that students might find useful themselves, such as a 1–100 chart.

The practices I've thus far mentioned make for teaching that supports all learners. Some specific students, like Ellie, Artie, and Marshall, need more specific interventions.

Approaches That Help Students Who Freeze Up at Math Time: Ellie's Story

Fourth grader Ellie—tall, outspoken, a lover of books, and a stunningly gifted writer—suffers terribly when it comes to math. She cannot do it. Facts she has been trying to memorize elude her, and her mathematical reasoning is oddly nonsensical. Worse, she has a tendency to freeze up completely when it comes time to tackle a problem.

Interestingly, the thinking Ellie so ably does to excel in reading and writing is exactly what she needs to excel in math. Part of Ellie's problem is that she does not seem to know that. As the years have gone by, her dislike for math has grown, and her ability to do it has in turn plummeted. Ellie's confidence in herself as a learner of mathematics is at an all-time low and getting worse with each math period she struggles through. I need to help her restore the confidence, interest, skills, and understandings she's missed along the way.

In order to tackle rather than avoid math, Ellie needs to become confident that her efforts will be successful. First, I address her negative feelings head-on. As her classmates buzz around her in varying degrees of math enthusiasm, she sits on the side, nearly immobile.

"What's up?" I ask Ellie.

"Nothing," she mumbles.

"Not sure what to do?" I prod.

Ellie nods, her eyes filling with tears. "Oh, I see," I say to her quietly, indicating that I'm about to share a secret. "You have brain freeze, and it's making you feel terrible. When people have brain freeze they start thinking things like, 'I can't to anything. All the other kids know what to do, and I don't. I must be stupid.' Are you thinking things like that?"

Ellie nods again.

"Ah, you definitely have brain freeze. Ellie, I know you can do this math. But as long as you are feeling so upset, it is really impossible to think. Why don't you take a little break? Read a book for a few minutes, and when you are feeling better, come find me."

Ellie returns ten minutes later, her eyes dried of tears. I sit with her, revisiting the lesson I did with the whole class earlier. Ellie is able to hear me a little better. It is just impossible for children to think or hear when they are so involved in the kind of negative thinking Ellie has been doing. It helps a child enormously to have her terrible thoughts acknowledged and then to be given a way to disengage from them. This is by no means the last time Ellie will suffer from brain freeze, but she has gained insight into what she is going through and a strategy for coping with it. Now that she has a tool for dealing with this crippling self-doubt, we are at a place where I can begin helping Ellie with math.

I want to help Ellie see that mathematics is, above all, about thinking. Like literacy, in which she excels, mathematics is about making sense of the world. Ellie is great at making sense of things: making relevant connections, drawing on prior knowledge and experience, and using strategies like visualizing and predicting. Comprehension is her strength; she just needs me to support her in using the skill to think about mathematics. I make a point of making sure she is tuned in when we address math comprehension skills as a class, and afterward

I debrief with Ellie. For example, when Ellie is stymied by a problem involving making change at the supermarket, I coach her to start by focusing on the situation. "Don't worry about whether you need to add or subtract, Ellie," I guide her. "Think about what's happening in the story. Visualize it. What would you do to make sure you get the right change from the cashier?" When Ellie can see the context that surrounds the math, she is better able to think it through.

Still, Ellie is hindered by her lack of fluency with basic facts and skills. Though I can help her apply her strong reading comprehension skills to math, she continues to get stuck whenever she comes to a problem like $9 + 8$. The next step in supporting Ellie requires a campaign to improve her fact fluency.

We begin to tackle this goal in a small group. I meet with Ellie and two classmates who also struggle with basic facts to determine which facts are still troubling them and to devise strategies for mastering these facts. This is not a one-size-fits-all proposition. For one of the struggling fourth graders, thinking about number relationships proves helpful: we discover that if Josh knows $8 + 8$, he can quickly do $8 + 9$, because it is just one more. For Ellie, flash cards do the trick. She loves the routine of repeatedly working her way through the deck and gains confidence from seeing herself do the cards more quickly and accurately each time. I'll admit, this is not my preferred method for working on mathematics, but Ellie isn't me. It is important to plan interventions based on what works for the child, not what suits the teacher's preferences. Though this is not the first time she has tried using flash cards to memorize math facts, it is the first time Ellie thinks it might work. She is determined. Through work at both school and home, Ellie masters these addition facts. She learns subtraction facts more easily once Ellie realizes she can look at a subtraction problem ($12 - 5 = ?$) as a missing-addend problem ($12 = 5 + ?$).

Ellie's eventual success in learning addition and subtraction facts is a big boost to her confidence and supports her subsequent math work. What's more, Ellie is not daunted by the prospect of mastering multiplication facts (a fourth-grade standard at my school). She knows she can do it.

Finally, I make an effort to involve Ellie's parents, especially her mother. Ellie's mother makes no secret of the fact that she shares her daughter's near phobia of mathematics. This otherwise successful woman declares herself as "missing the math gene." She celebrates Ellie's beautiful writing and identifies with her struggles in math. Ellie, in turn, identifies with her mother: *I, too, will succeed—as long as I avoid math.* For students like Ellie, mathematics seems to be a subject that they put up with when they have to take it; once they can make the choice, they drop math subjects as soon as possible.

I approach Ellie's mom directly during our parent-teacher conference. I start by asking her to share her experience: "Ellie doesn't have much confidence in her ability to do math. What was math like for you? Did you find it hard?" Ellie's mom shares her miserable math experiences, one story after another, each one prefaced by her claim that she lacks the math gene. When it is my turn to talk, I immediately debunk the math-gene myth. Ellie is not missing the gene for math. Instead, I suggest, kids are amazingly tuned into our attitudes. Is it possible, I suggest, that Ellie has picked up on her mom's math phobia?

I follow up our conversation by personally inviting Ellie's mom to our school's math night for parents. This event is a time for teachers to share with parents their philosophy about mathematics and their approaches for teaching it. Even more importantly, each math night for parents includes opportunities for adults to do math; we present the same kinds of mathematics lessons we teach their children. Parents play math games and work cooperatively on multistep problems. They use manipulatives and write about their thinking. Every year we hear from parents who fear and hate mathematics that they had a different experience at math night for parents. *I wish I learned math this way* is a frequent response on the feedback forms. I predict that Ellie's mom will have a similar positive experience, and that she may, as a result, be less likely to discredit math and her ability to do it.

I am lucky to have a well-organized math event to invite parents to attend. Teachers whose schools do not host such an event have found creative alternatives. One option is to have math mornings: designated school mornings on which parents are invited to attend class and do math with their children. In teaching literacy, we often invite parents to publishing parties to celebrate their children's writing. A useful side effect is parent education. We celebrate math and help parents better understand how we are teaching it when we invite them to come look through their children's math work and play a game or participate in some other math-related activity with their children.

The approaches I've thus far mentioned have been very helpful to Ellie, and though math still does not hold a candle to reading and writing in Ellie's affections, we are all pleased to see that she is on her way to becoming a confident and competent math student. She no longer dreads math time and even admits to enjoying it at times. She easily understood the math she studied in fifth grade and reportedly even likes math in middle school!

Approaches That Help Students Who Find School Difficult: Artie's Story

Artie is another puzzle. A big boy for his age—with a humor and temper to match—Artie, unlike Ellie, finds just about everything in fourth grade hard. (He takes refuge in his size and his impressive anger, which hold people—even me—at bay.) Artie can never find a book that interests him, can never stick with a writing topic, and can never make sense of math. It is hard to get him to write more than a few sentences, and even then, most of his spelling is approximate (or as he puts it, *wrong*).

Socially, Artie doesn't get along with other kids; he has a tremendous chip on his shoulder and takes even the most casual of comments ("Could you move? I can't reach the paper.") as a personal insult ("She said I was fat!"). He does, however, have enormous pride in his beautiful handwriting and continually intrigues me with his strange and elaborate drawings of futuristic knights and dragons. In addition, his adoring parents are thoughtful and supportive, and they desperately want to help him.

In debating about how to help Artie succeed in math, I focus on what is helping him in literacy learning. What I learn is that Artie needs to do lots of work that he can complete with ease. Not only is this key in building skills and understanding, but it also helps develop his confidence and engagement. Children like Artie do not have a whole lot of tolerance for failure. It is terribly difficult for Artie to stick with something when it is hard for him. No one needs to use the bathroom or go to the drinking fountain more than Artie, and it is always possible to pick a fight with a classmate. If all else fails, he'll push his work away, announcing, "This is dumb!"

It is critical that I adjust the difficulty of a day's work so that Artie can handle it without experiencing overwhelming frustration. This might mean choosing more manageable numbers or eliminating a step or two in multistep problems. It might also mean asking Artie to create two symmetrical designs instead of four. Most often, for Artie, it means getting him into a math game as often as possible. Artie loves games, and it is usually possible for me to ensure that there is a simpler version for those that are too complex. The structure of the math curriculum also supports this: I often offer children activity choices for learning about such topics as fractions, multiplication, or measurement. These choices almost always include a game, and I almost always steer Artie toward it. Easy games in particular keep Artie attentive. As an added bonus, when Artie is busy playing a game he excels at, he also has the opportunity to improve his relations with his peers.

Next, I make use of Artie's excellent handwriting. He yearns to be seen in a good light. I want to catch Artie doing something right, and I want to do it in math class. I find an opportunity when the class is working on recording multiplication strategies. One of the challenges of having kids invent their own algorithms is that they don't automatically come up with clear ways to record them. Unless my students have an opportunity to work on developing strategies for organizing their thinking, their work can be difficult to decipher— even for themselves. When the class is focusing on organization, Artie is working on a splitting strategy for multiplying double-digit numbers by single-digit numbers. On a particularly successful day, I keep the numbers small and easy for Artie and focus his attention on organizing his work. The results are gorgeous. In his lovely handwriting, Artie has neatly listed the steps he took in splitting factors, multiplying parts, and combining products. His answer is correct, too—success is starting to happen.

The next day I share Artie's work with the class and invite Artie to talk about what he had done. This doesn't happen every day. It is time that Artie stop being the boy who is always in trouble and start being an important contributor to our class. Today the assignment is to revisit the work students did yesterday. "Try to make it as clearly organized as Artie's," I say. Throughout the morning, classmates come to

Artie for advice. He is extraordinarily proud to be an example for others to follow.

This is the real beginning of Artie's growing success in math. Now that his confidence and attitude are improving, I need to slowly increase his tolerance for frustration. It helps to think of this as a series of separate tasks. I am explicit with Artie about each of them: "Today we are going to work on trying something more challenging. It might take you longer to finish, so I am going to help you stick with it by checking in with you at least three times." Or "Today's assignment might be tricky. If you make a mistake, come find me so we can talk about what you are going to learn from your mistake instead of getting mad at yourself." Or "Today we are going to work on getting more work done. It is ten o'clock now. I am going to come see you when it is ten after ten and we will talk about how much work you got done."

Artie has made steady progress in fourth-grade math. He isn't cured of his difficulties at school, and his parents and I agree that he continues to need support. However, he has developed a better attitude and his skills and understandings have definitely improved.

Approaches That Help Students with Learning Disabilities: Marshall's Story

Then there is Marshall. An amiable boy who easily makes friends, Marshall began receiving special education services in third grade when it became apparent that his achievement was well below his potential. Because of the challenges his learning disabilities present, Marshall has difficulty internalizing conceptual material, such as place value, holding facts in his long-term memory, and sequencing and organizing his thinking on paper. A strong visual learner, Marshall does best with tasks that involve the manipulation of geometric shapes. He is successfully mainstreamed but requires intensive intervention. He has the support of several specialists—a special education teacher, a speech and language specialist, and an occupational therapist. And because Marshall is so behind his classmates in his conceptual understanding and skills, he needs a highly adaptable math curriculum.

The temptation with students like Marshall is to leave them to the specialists. It would be easy for me to leave his math instruction with his special education teacher, Marcia Kimmel. But Marcia and I both know that though he definitely needs special attention, pulling him from class daily to work with Marcia would further isolate Marshall from his classmates. Plus, he would miss everything that was happening in fourth grade. Therefore, Marcia arranges her schedule so that instead of pulling Marshall out at math time, she pushes in. She sits by Marshall during the whole-group lesson, quietly helping him interpret what the other students and I are talking about and helping him engage with other students when it is time to talk. When the other children get started on the day's task, Marcia works with a small group of children who need support and is able to help me provide Marshall with an adapted version of the day's work. Sometimes the adjustment is minor and sometimes it is quite extensive. Because Marshall works more easily with shapes than numbers, geometry activities rarely need changes, while number activities sometimes require a complete overhaul in operations (for example, Marshall might work on mastering addition facts while his classmates master multiplication).

Even when Marcia is in the room to support Marshall, it is critical that I stay involved in his work. Marshall is still my student and my responsibility, and I have the best overall understanding of the math he needs to do. The best way to help Marshall is via a thorough and well-communicated collaboration.

Marcia and I also work to make math less frustrating and more rewarding for Marshall. Like Artie, Marshall also needs an abundance of easy math experiences. He really enjoys simple math games, and he makes a great buddy to a first grader who needs practice with sums of ten. The opportunity to know more than other students, even younger ones, increases Marshall's confidence, and he takes pride in teaching the younger children games like *Tens Go Fish* and *Concentration for Tens,* in which students look for pairs of cards that add up to ten.

Finally, Marcia and I work with Marshall's family to make sure he is developing the kind of prior knowledge necessary to succeed in math. Prior knowledge plays a clearly important role in reading and writing and an equally significant role in mathematics. Prior knowledge establishes a context for learning; students need that context to understand new concepts. When students begin exploring multiplicative thinking, they draw from their prior knowledge that people tend to group things and often need to count these groups. They also draw on prior experience with skips counting and what they understand about addition.

Marshall often fails to draw on the prior knowledge necessary to make sense of the math we are doing. Marcia and I need to help him connect his everyday life experiences—grocery shopping, baking cookies, collecting coins, and divvying up toy cars—with his classroom math. We make a point of suggesting math-rich, everyday activities to Marshall's family and provide as many of these activities as we can to help Marshall in school, taking care to explicitly make the connection between the real-life context and the math embedded in it. Hoping to give him experiences we can draw on when we begin work on division, for example, we take Marshall to the corner store to buy snacks for the class, then give him the task of fairly sharing the snacks with his classmates.

Though we suspect that mathematics will always present some difficulty to Marshall, Marshall's special education teacher and I are committed to meeting him where he is and moving him as far forward as we possibly can. We are gratified by his interest, his effort, and even his willingness to withstand frustrations. Marshall continues to succeed in math on his own terms, and we continue to keep our eyes open for new opportunities to help him.

The Whole Picture

The successes I've described here are not magic. Though they all made tremendous gains, Ellie, Artie, and Marshall—and a few of their classmates—still struggle in some aspects of mathematics. Ellie ended the year successfully doing the math her more math-avid peers were doing, but I doubt she will ever love it as they do. Artie and Marshall, on the other hand, are still below grade level. They will continue to need the support of expert teachers. However, all three students are succeeding in their own ways, and their confidence has definitely improved. These children have also succeeded in teaching me. Here are some of the invaluable lessons I've learned:

◆ *There is no one best way to teach math.* Rote memorization is the key to Ellie learning her facts, while Marshall needs alternatives to the standard algorithm to make any headway in addition. The best way to teach math is the one that helps individual students learn it.

◆ *Confidence is paramount.* Just as reading and writing must be rewarding, so must doing mathematics. If the result is frustration and feeling stupid, students will stop making an effort.

◆ *Professional development is important for teaching all students.* If we are committed to finding the right approach, strategy, activity, or game that each of our struggling students needs, we need professional support. We also need to understand what underlies our students' challenges; this means we need to continually take steps to educate ourselves on the math we are doing and to understand it inside out.

◆ *Everyone has the potential to understand math.* Finally, we must continue to believe that we can help *all* children understand mathematics.

FROM READING TO MATH TO YOUR CLASSROOM

1. *Do you think you have bought into the math-gene myth, perhaps without even realizing it? If so, how can you change your beliefs and attitude, and how can you project to your students that you think they can all do math?*

2. *Do you have students like Ellie, Artie, or Marshall? If so, what might you do to begin lessening their struggles and exploiting their strengths? Try to write out a step-by-step plan for helping each individual advance.*

3. *Do you have students with different challenges? What might you do to address their needs?*

Appendix: From Reading to Math to Your Classroom

Chapter 1

1. What are strategies for teaching reading that you feel particularly confident with that you can adapt for teaching math?
2. What are aspects of math learning or teaching that you already enjoy? If you feel there are no enjoyable aspects, how might you find a way to fall in love with math?
3. Can you think of any lessons your students have taught you about math? Have you been open to letting them teach you?

Chapter 2

1. What do you think it means to be fluent in math? What signs of fluency can you look for in students?
2. What math contexts are you already providing students? What new ones can you add to your classroom?
3. What are the important Tier 3 words for the unit you're currently teaching? How can you help students learn this vocabulary?

Chapter 3

1. Think of a math unit you teach. How could you help students use the comprehension strategies discussed in this chapter to learn the content of that unit?
2. How will you know if students are making meaning in math? What can you do if they are not making meaning?
3. What other questions could you ask students in math to help them get started, get unstuck, check their work, or go deeper?
4. How can you rephrase questions you commonly ask so that you don't know the answers before asking the questions?

5. How will you know when students are comprehending math? What signs will you look for?

Chapter 4

1. What do you think are the essential elements of a successful reading classroom? Are they essential in the math classroom as well? If so, how can you make sure they are present?
2. What might you do to increase your knowledge of the math you teach, the curriculum you use, and your students?
3. What are some other ways to integrate math learning into the rest of your day?

Chapter 5

1. How will you transition to using a math workshop approach?
2. What other components of your literacy workshop might be transferable to a math workshop?
3. What rules and expectations would you need to have in place in order to have an effective math workshop?
4. How can you maintain a good balance of independent and collaborative work in math class?
5. How might you conduct math shares in your class?

Chapter 6

1. Have you ever tried conferring with students about math? How did it go? How could it have gone better?
2. How can you help students self-assess their math learning, and what do you want them to focus on when assessing themselves?
3. What do you consider to be fact mastery?
4. How can you help students define success in different stages of their math learning?

Chapter 7

1. Do you think you have bought into the math-gene myth, perhaps without even realizing it? If so, how can you change your beliefs and attitude, and how can you project to your students that you think they can *all* do math?
2. Do you have students like Ellie, Artie, or Marshall? If so, what might you do to begin lessening their struggles and exploiting their strengths? Try to write out a step-by-step plan for helping each individual advance.
3. Do you have students with different challenges? What might you do to address their needs?

References

Akers, Joan, Claryce Evans, Megan Murray, and Cornelia Tierney. 1998. *Name That Portion: Fractions, Decimals, and Percents*. Menlo Park, CA: Dale Seymour.

Allington, Richard. 2006. *What Really Matters for Struggling Readers: Designing Research-Based Programs*. Boston: Allyn and Bacon.

Allington, Richard, and Patricia Cunningham. 2006. *Schools That Work: Where All Children Read and Write*. Boston: Allyn and Bacon.

Anderson, Carl. 2000. *How's It Going? A Practical Guide to Conferring with Student Writers*. Portsmouth, NH: Heinemann.

Bear, Donald, Marcia Invernizzi, Shane Templeton, and Francine Johnson. 2004. *Words Their Way: Word Study for Phonics, Vocabulary, and Spelling Instruction*. Upper Saddle River, NJ: Pearson Education.

Beck, Isabel, Margaret McKeown, and Linda Kucan. 2002. *Bringing Words to Life: Robust Vocabulary Instruction*. New York: Guilford.

Brown, Hazel, and Brian Cambourne. 1987. *Read and Retell: A Strategy for the Whole Language/Natural Learning Classroom*. Portsmouth, NH: Heinemann.

Burns, Marilyn. 2007. *About Teaching Mathematics: A K–8 Resource*. 3d ed. Sausalito, CA: Math Solutions.

Calkins, Lucy McCormick. 2001. *The Art of Teaching Reading*. New York: Addison-Wesley Educational Publishers.

Carle, Eric. 1972. *Rooster's Off to See the World*. New York: F. Watts.

Chandler, David. 2005. *Exploring the Night Sky with Binoculars*. Springville, CA: David Chandler Company.

Chapin, Suzanne, and Art Johnson. 2006. *Math Matters: Understanding the Math You Teach, Grades K–8.* 2d ed. Sausalito, CA: Math Solutions.

Chapin, Suzanne, Catherine O'Connor, and Nancy Canavan Anderson. 2009. *Classroom Discussions: Using Math Talk to Help Students Learn, Grades K–6.* 2d ed. Sausalito, CA: Math Solutions.

Encyclopedia Britannica Online Encyclopedia. n.d. www.britannica.com/ EBchecked/topic/369194/mathematics.

Fosnot, Catherine Twomey, and Maarten Dolk. 2001. *Young Mathematicians at Work: Constructing Multiplication and Division.* Portsmouth, NH: Heinemann.

Fountas, Irene, and Gay Su Pinnell. 1996. *Guided Reading: Good First Teaching for All Children.* Portsmouth, NH: Heinemann.

Harvey, Stephanie, and Anne Goudvis. 2000. *Strategies That Work: Teaching Comprehension to Enhance Understanding.* York, ME: Stenhouse.

Jacobs, Heidi Hayes. 2006. *Active Literacy Across the Curriculum: Strategies for Reading, Writing, Speaking and Listening.* Larchmont, NY: Eye on Education.

Johnson, Peter. 1997. *Knowing Literacy: Constructivist Literacy Assessment.* York, ME: Stenhouse.

Keene, Ellin Oliver, and Susan Zimmermann. 1997. *Mosaic of Thought: Teaching Comprehension in a Reader's Workshop.* Portsmouth, NH: Heinemann.

Kinsella, Kate, and Kevin Feldman. 2005. *Narrowing the Language Gap: The Case for Explicit Vocabulary Instruction.* http://teacher.scholastic.com/ products/authors/pdfs/narrowing_the_gap.pdf.

Lewis, C. S. 1950. *The Lion, the Witch, and the Wardrobe.* New York: Harper Trophy.

Mencken, H. L. 1949. *A Mencken Chrestomanthy.* New York: Vintage.

Merriam-Webster's Online Dictionary. n.d. www.merriam-webster.com/ dictionary/workshop.

Mitchell, W. J. T. 1986. *Iconology: Image, Text, Ideology.* Chicago: University of Chicago Press.

Mooney, Margaret. 1995. *Developing Life-Long Readers.* Wellington, NZ: Learning Media.

Murray, Miki. 2004. *Teaching Mathematics Vocabulary in Context.* Portsmouth, NH: Heinemann.

New Zealand Ministry of Education. 1997. *Reading for Life: The Learner as a Reader.* Wellington, NZ: Learning Media.

Pandell, Karen. 2003. *I Love You, Sun, I Love You, Moon*. New York: Grosset and Dunlap.

Pressley, Michael, Richard Allington, Ruth Wharton-McDonald, Cathy Collins Block, and Lesley Mandel Morrow. 2001. *Learning to Read: Lessons from Exemplary First-Grade Classrooms*. New York: Guilford.

Ray, Katie Wood, with Lester Laminack. 2001. *The Writing Workshop: Working Through the Hard Parts (and They're All Hard Parts)*. Urbana, IL: National Council of Teachers of English.

Rhodes, Richard. 1995. *The Making of the Atomic Bomb*. New York: Simon and Schuster.

Routman, Regie. 2000. *Conversations: Strategies for Teaching, Learning, and Evaluating*. Portsmouth, NH: Heinemann.

Saphier, Jon, and Robert Gower. 1997. *The Skillful Teacher: Building Your Teaching Skills*. Acton, MA: Research for Better Teaching.

Schuster, Lainie, and Nancy Canavan Anderson. 2005. *Good Questions for Math Teaching: Why Ask Them and What to Ask, Grades 5–8*. Sausalito, CA: Math Solutions.

Smith, Frank. 2003. *Unspeakable Acts, Unnatural Practices: Fallacies in "Scientific" Reading Instruction*. Portsmouth, NH: Heinemann.

Snowball, Diane. 2005. *Teaching Comprehension: An Interactive Professional Development Course*. CD-ROM. Port Washington, NY: A.U.S.S.I.E. Interactive.

Snowball, Diane, and Faye Bolton. 1999. *Spelling K–8: Planning and Teaching*. York, ME: Stenhouse.

Tierney, Cornelia, and Mary Berle-Carman. 1998. *Fair Shares: Fractions*. Menlo Park, CA: Dale Seymour.

Tierney, Cornelia, Mark Ogonowski, Andee Rubin, and Susan Jo Russell. 1998. *Different Shapes, Equal Pieces: Fractions and Area*. Menlo Park, CA: Dale Seymour.

Wilder, Laura Ingalls. 1940. *The Long Winter*. New York: Harper Trophy.

Index

B

basic math facts, mastery of, 112–15

Beck, Isabel, 25
Bringing Words to Life: Robust Vocabulary Instruction, 25–26

Berle-Carman, Mary (*Fair Shares: Fractions*), 124–25

Block, Cathy C. (*Learning to Read: Lessons from Exemplary First-Grade Classrooms*), 52

Bolton, Faye, 25
Spelling K–8: Planning and Teaching, 25

book clubs, in literacy workshops, 73

brain freeze, helping learners with math, 125–29

Bringing Words to Life: Robust Vocabulary Instruction (Beck, McKeown, and Kucan), 25–26

Burns, Marilyn, 48
About Teaching Mathematics: A K–8 Resource, 17–18, 47

C

calendars, integrating math with, 63

Calkins, Lucy (*Art of Teaching Reading, The*), 76

Carle, Eric (*Rooster's Off to See the World*), 80, 96

Carlyle, Ann, 39

centers, in literacy workshops, 73

Chandler, David (*Exploring the Night Sky with Binoculars*), 46

Chapin, Suzanne
Classroom Discussions: Using Math Talk to Help Students Learn, Grades K–6, 94–95, 107–8
Math Matters: Understanding the Math You Teach, Grades K–8, 64, 113

checking work, questions for, 41–42

Classroom Discussions: Using Math Talk to Help Students Learn, Grades

K–6 (Chapin, O'Connor, and Anderson), 94–95, 107–8

classroom environment that supports all students, creating, 124–25

classroom management
environment, designing, 55–56
in successful classrooms, 53–54

classrooms
manipulatives, fostering independent use of, 56–57
planning, using curriculum for effective, 64–66
print-rich math environments, creating, 57–60
routines, integrating math with daily classroom, 62–63
scheduling and pacing lessons, 61–63
students succeed, creating classrooms that help all, 60–61
successful, attributes of, 52–54
unsuccessful, attributes of, 54–55

comprehension, math
checking work, questions for, 41–42
deeper, questions for going, 42–43
monitoring, 49–50
questioning, as strategy, 38–47
repairing understanding, 49–50
started, questions for getting, 39–40
summarizing, as strategy, 47–49
synthesizing, as strategy, 47–49
tapping prior knowledge, as strategy, 35–38
teaching, 34–51
unstuck, questions for getting, 40–41
visualizing (*see* visualizing)

comprehension, reading
inferring, as strategy, 32
monitoring, as strategy, 33–34
questioning, as strategy, 31–32
repairing understanding, as strategy, 33–34
steps to teaching, 34
strategies for reading, 30–34
summarizing, as strategy, 32–33
surge in interest in, 30–31